A 1970s
Childhood

A 1970s Childhood

*From Glam Rock
to Happy Days*

DEREK TAIT

Front cover photograph: Elizabeth II's Silver Jubilee, 1977. A children's tea party in a street in Horley © Mary Evans Picture Library/Alamy

First published 2011

Reprinted 2011. 2012, 2013, 2015, 2017

The History Press
The Mill, Brimscombe Port
Stroud, Gloucestershire, GL5 2QG
www.thehistorypress.co.uk

British Library Cataloguing in Publication Data.
A catalogue record for this book is available from the British Library.

ISBN 978 0 7524 6344 5

Typesetting and origination by The History Press
Printed and bound by CPI Group (UK) Ltd, Croydon, CRO 4YY

CONTENTS

Acknowledgements

Most of the photos that appear in this book are family photos or images of items that I've collected over the years. Thanks go to Brandon Coombes (Radio One Roadshow photo), Janice Drew Crotts (the platform shoes photo), Alan Gold (1970s checked trouser advert), John Hudson (the Tom Baker photo), Klaus Hiltscher (for the Noddy Holder and Hugh Cornwell photos), Georg Holderied (photo of calculators), NASA/courtesy of nasaimages.org (for the Apollo 14 patch), Steve Johnson (various photos taken around Plymouth in the 1970s), Jason Liebig (the Fonz sticker), Gillian Long (for the Silver Jubilee photo), Mike McCarthy (for the Planet of the Apes poster) and Matt Sefton (for the skateboarding photos).

I have tried to trace the copyright holders of all photos and illustrations used and I apologise to anyone who I haven't mentioned.

One

AT HOME

It seems odd that 1970 is over forty years ago now and yet I remember exactly what I was doing on 1 January 1970. We were still on our Christmas holidays, it was a sunny day, and my brother Alan and I went out for the day to see what we could get up to. I was 8 at the time and Alan was 13. In those days, dogs just wandered the street, many with no collars, and then returned home in the evening for their tea. As kids, we got to know most of the dogs in the area. Anyhow, on this day we came across a dog while playing on the nearby football pitch and he followed us around all day. Some other kids told us that his name was 'Skip' and he regularly played with kids in the area. We spent the day playing in the nearby fields, close to the school I attended, got some sweets from the local shop and ended up eating them in our den which was built from material taken from the local building site. When we first moved into our street in the late 1960s, the houses at the far end were still being built. There were never any fences around building sites in those days and we spent a lot of our time running along walls, climbing up planks in the half-built houses that had no stairs and looking for materials to build dens. This included sheets of corrugated iron, wooden poles, chicken wire and just about anything we could get our hands on. We had dens all over the place. One, which was in the woods near our house, was an old air-raid shelter. We'd made a door for it and had even found a pair of armchairs about a mile away that somebody had dumped.

Anyway, back to 1 January and the afternoon we spent with Skip in our den before exploring the woods. At the time, there were pigs kept there in little chicken wire pens. I never knew whom they belonged to, but looking back it seems strange that someone should have kept pigs in the woods near a housing estate.

We wandered back up to the shops and I remember we were told off several times because Skip kept chasing after cars. 'Control your dog!' people shouted. 'It's not our dog!' we answered, but no one took any notice. By the time we went home for our tea, Skip had decided to return home too. We'd had a great day. I thought I would see Skip again the next day but we never saw him again. Maybe he chased one too many cars.

The reason I remember 1 January so well is because my mum and dad had bought me a Walt Disney diary for Christmas and I would write in it as neatly as possible, recording what we'd done in the day. This lasted for about three weeks before my writing got worse, and by February I'd stopped writing in it altogether. Although it was thrown out many years ago, I wish I still had it. After all, it was because of the diary that I'll forever remember what I did on that first day of 1970.

I remember two other presents that I got for Christmas and they were *The Beano* and *The Dandy* annuals. I've still got them and look at them occasionally. I must know them off by heart. I used to get *The Beano*, I think, every Wednesday and Alan got the *Valiant*. There were lots of long forgotten comics that I can remember from back then, including *The Hotspur*, *The Tiger*, *TV Century 21*, *Look and Learn* and *TV Comic*. I never liked *Look and Learn* much because it was too educational. What sort of comic didn't have a character like Biffo the Bear? These were the comics you had to read in class if it was a rainy day and you couldn't go out at playtime.

Later on, there were other comics I got regularly like *Whizzer and Chips* and *Cor!!* They always came with free gifts such as plastic chocolate biscuits to give to your dad or plastic liquorice and other jokes. I also loved the American comics, especially *Superman*. There were some strange adverts in these comics, including one announcing, 'You too could have a body like Charles Atlas!' (even though he'd been dead for thirty years) and another promoting 'Sea Monkeys'. The advert showed monkeys in a fish bowl doing all sorts of acrobatic tricks. That looked fantastic to me and, when a British comic offered the same thing as a free gift, I bought it and poured the contents of the packet into a bowl of water and waited for my monkeys to appear. About ten days later, what I

Dad travelled all over the world with the Navy and would send us back postcards and stamps from wherever he went. My favourite was the one of the apes in Gibraltar! I've still got the postcards and it's very interesting reading them all today.

actually ended up with was a bowl of shrimps! Not a Sea Monkey in sight!

Living right beside the woods, we would be woken up by the dawn chorus – thousands of birds singing as soon as the sun came up. There were a lot more birds around in the 1970s than there are now. The milkman and postman would always come at the same time every morning. Quite often, we would find the silver-foil milk bottle tops pecked in by the blue tits. Occasionally, the milkman would accidentally leave Gold Top, which was thick and creamy, instead of the ordinary milk, and we would have it on our cornflakes. There was no milk in cartons back then and certainly no skimmed or semi-skimmed milk. Sometimes, if Alan and I were up early in the holidays or on a Saturday, we would catch the milkman and buy a pint of milk off him.

Mum worked in the nearby newsagents and dad was away a lot of the time in the Navy. It was handy mum working in the newsagents. If we were passing or coming home from school, she'd give us sweets or lollies.

At home, Alan and I slept in a bunk bed and he would tell me stories at night. Some mornings, we would wake up and there would be cows asleep in the garden from the many nearby farms. Today, forty years later, with all the new housing estates, it's hard to imagine.

We had pictures and posters all over the walls. Some were of pop stars cut out of the music papers that Alan would get and there were also a few of footballers. Alan supported Tottenham Hotspur and I supported Leeds United, mainly because Jackie Charlton played for them.

1970 was the year of the World Cup and I vividly recall Alan and me staying up late one night to watch the final England match in May 1970. Whenever we were out in the car, we always made sure that dad visited the Esso garage so that we could get our World Cup medallions, each with a player's face embossed on it. Because of this, I remember every member of the 1970s squad which included Bobby Moore, Alan Ball, Geoff Hurst, Jeff Astle, Gordon Banks, Colin Bell, Peter Bonetti, Bobby Charlton, Jack Charlton, Allan Clarke, Terry Cooper, Colin Harvey, Emlyn Hughes, Norman Hunter, Mick Jones, Brian Labone, Francis Lee, Paul Madeley, Ian Moore, Alan Mullery, Henry Newton, Keith Newton, Alan Oakes, Martin Peters, Paul Reaney, Peter Shilton, Peter Thompson and Tommy Wright. What a team! How did we lose? I also remember Alan and me having World Cup scrapbooks, collecting bubblegum cards and me even having Jackie Charlton on my pencil case. I didn't even like football!

Everyone was singing *Back Home*, the song recorded by the team, which was number one for three weeks. Indeed, the 1970s World Cup is the one I'll always recall most vividly because everyone was so into it at the time.

I loved all the music papers that Alan got, not just for the colour posters in the middle but also for the adverts in the back which mostly consisted of people selling stuff or requesting material on their favourite pop stars. For a while, I had a pen friend who was 14 when I was 11. She collected stuff on Cat Stevens and I collected stuff on The Monkees (my favourite band at the beginning of the 1970s). I didn't want her to know that I was only 11 because I thought that she wouldn't write so I used to get Alan to write my letters for me. I probably had to bribe him. In the end, Alan got fed up and I resorted to writing in my scruffy handwriting (she must have noticed the difference) before, like most pen friends, it all fizzled out.

Nobody that we knew had a telephone and we didn't have one either. If mum wanted to get in contact with dad when he was away in the Navy, we would have to walk to the nearest phone box. There used to be a lot more around then as everyone used them. I think that it was 2p for a local call and 10p for a national call. When we eventually did get a phone, it was wired up incorrectly so all that we could pick up was the radio! It was soon fixed, but in those days everyone shared a line (a party line) so you would quite often pick up the phone and someone else would be

Our old telephone. They came in a range of colours; ours was in light mustard.

on there talking. There was a service called 'Dial-A-Disc' where you could dial sixteen and listen to the latest chart hits. You couldn't imagine anyone doing it nowadays but it was the equivalent of looking up your favourite song on YouTube today.

I seem to remember it snowing a lot when I was a kid. I remember once it snowed all week and we went along to the building site at the end of the road. We called it 'Mount Everest' then because there was a big slope from the site heading down to the road. We would get bits of card or

My I-Spy badge, which everyone got when you joined the *Daily Mail*'s I-Spy club. We had hours of fun spotting various animals and objects.

wood that the builders had left lying around and use them as sledges to slide down the hill. We would also tie rope to the scaffold around the building and lower it down the hill and then climb up it like we were proper mountaineers. We knew the exact time when the builders went home and after school we would go to the site just to run and jump off walls or to see what we could find. All the kids did it. There never seemed to be any health and safety rules back then. Nobody ever caught us and if one of the builders did return, we'd just run off. They didn't seem to have been much bothered anyway. Sometimes we would mix up a bit of cement and do a bit of bricklaying. Everything was just left lying around!

We would make our own bows and arrows and fire at targets (they were never very good) and make catapults for firing at tin cans. We also all had water pistols, which were great in the long hot summers, and potato guns, which we always fired at our friends. I remember dad bringing us some great guns back from Spain one year. They fired caps and looked just like the real thing – just the sort of thing that 007 would have! It's funny to think that you could take items like that through customs in those days without anyone questioning it. We pretended to be James Bond all summer, but the guns were finally ruined when we took them to the beach and we got sand in them.

We all had I-Spy books, which were linked with a column featuring Chief I-Spy (a Red Indian) in the *Daily Mail*. They involved looking out for things such as cars, birds, dogs, zoo animals, things in the countryside, things in the woods – the titles were endless. I must have learned all about butterflies, birds and animals through books like these and by collecting various Brooke Bond cards.

I'm certain that we had one I-Spy book that featured animal tracks, and when it snowed Alan and I would go out looking to see what strange animals and birds had been wandering around during the night. I'm sure we prob-ably thought that we'd found the tracks of foxes, deer and other animals, but thinking about it now they were more likely just the tracks of cats and dogs. We even left our own paw prints in the snow by putting four fingers together and pressing down on them. To us, that looked just like a wild animal print. By watching cartoons like Scooby Doo, I really believed that we might come across a Yeti or some other weird creature! Your imagination is fantastic when you're a kid.

At about the same time, Tuf brought out shoes which had paw prints on the soles so that you could leave a trail as you walked. They also brought out a pair which featured a compass in the heel. All the kids pestered their mums for these new shoes but they had one major drawback – they always gave you blisters. Clark's shoes, which were their main rivals, had none of the gimmicks of Tuf but were certainly a lot more comfortable. They did bring out one pair that all the kids liked – Commandos!

Alan eventually moved into his own bedroom so I had a room to myself. Being the 1970s, Alan had purple wallpaper with leather effect tiles around his bed. He also had two Pace posters of Marc Bolan on the walls that mum had brought back from the shop were she worked. Alan loved T. Rex and Marc Bolan and, once mum had left for work during our summer holidays, he would blast me out of bed with *Metal Guru* and *Get it On*. All I wanted to do was lie in! My room had dark blue wallpaper and Pace posters of Alias Smith and Jones. We all loved that show. Later, I had posters of Alvin Stardust, some taken straight from the pages of *Look-in*.

We all watched the TV together in the living room (there was only one TV in the house so we all had to watch the same programmes). If someone wanted to watch the other side, they'd have to go to a friend's house. Alan used to like *Top of the Pops*, but there was always something on the other side that I liked watching. I think that he won in the end.

All mums seemed to knit in the 1970s and we must have got used to the clicking as we watched the telly. There was a knitting pattern for everything (including Starsky's jumper) and there were shops just selling wool and little else. All the kids at school had jumpers knitted by their mums; it's funny how knitting has since come back into fashion.

Mum would crochet a lot and we had a lot of crocheted blankets. Crochet jackets were fashionable for women and mum made them for the people who worked in the shop. Eventually, they all had one!

Every mum seemed to run a catalogue. The ones that I remember were Great Universal, Littlewoods, Freemans and Janet Frazer. I'm sure that there were many more. You could get something from the catalogue and pay it off gradually every week.

We used to love the catalogues coming out so that we could go straight to the toy section and see what new toys were due in the shops. I loved looking at all the annuals, which appeared in the catalogues long before they appeared anywhere else.

Money seemed to go a long way back then. If you were a kid and had a pound note, which was 20s, you were considered well off. In the pre-decimal days of 1970 and 1971, most kids had a few old pennies and halfpennies to spend on sweets and other things. Two shillings (a florin) seemed a lot of money to a boy in those days. I remember that I found an old woman's purse by the playing fields one day and it had her address on it so I took it back to her. She was really pleased and wanted to give me a shilling as a reward. I'd have loved the shilling but turned her down. Later, she gave the shilling to my mum up at the shop and insisted that

This photo shows one of my favourite pastimes as a boy – climbing trees! I'm wearing my favourite purple t-shirt, my brown corduroys and my school gym shoes. I remember our dog Shep wearing that jacket when we dressed him up as Superdog for the day!

An old £1 note.

I had it. It doesn't sound much but a shilling seemed a lot in pre-decimal days.

I loved all the power cuts of the 1970s. We would be watching the telly and suddenly the power would go and we were stuck there in the dark. We always had lots of candles to hand (I think my mum's still got them somewhere!) and there was something nice and cosy about it. Sometimes we would listen to the radio, if it had batteries, or play cards or other games. I remember once walking back from seeing a friend at the nearby flats and all the lights went out behind me and I had to walk home in total darkness. It was very eerie.

All kids seemed to have scraped knees in the 1970s from various adventures, which included jumping off buildings and garages, climbing trees, falling off bikes and roller skates, playing 'It' and 'British Bulldog' and general falls while rushing about.

We had dens all over the woods. We had a good one just behind the house in the woods and the undergrowth. In the summer, the ferns came above my head and it seemed well hidden. Our air-raid shelter den, deep in the woods, mentioned earlier, was perhaps our best den. Several kids would meet up there and we even had our own furniture. We had a stack of old 78rpm records in case the den came under attack. We used to throw them around like Frisbees. Of course, they smashed on impact.

One day we went to visit the den but it had been completely wrecked (which happened often). Even our armchairs were pulled apart. Nowadays if you saw a den in the woods you would probably call the police, but back then all the kids built them.

The council eventually took the air-raid shelter that had been there for years away and there's no sign of it today. I remember one summer when we had more ambitious plans for a den. We cleared a bit of the woodland behind our houses and made a fence out of old string. All the kids in the street seemed to be involved. I can't remember it ever coming to much but I remember us all lying in the ferns looking skywards, daydreaming in the sun. My den-building days only seemed to last until I was about 11 years old. Once we all went to secondary school, no one ever seemed to build dens again.

We all had Observer books and would try to spot everything that was in them. The three that I remember having were on Birds, Astronomy (written by Patrick Moore) and Dogs. I got very interested in Astronomy because of that little Observer book, and later in the 1970s, when Dixons brought out their own telescope for £19.99, mum and dad bought me one for my birthday. It was excellent and I would spend ages in the garden looking at the moon, the stars and the rings around Saturn. Unfortunately, I took

Dad's birthday in about 1973. Everything in the photo looks very 1970s, including the wallpaper, the crockery, the salt and pepper set, my tank top and purple shirt and dad's sideburns.

it apart later to clean it and it was never quite the same again.

Having your haircut in the early seventies meant going to the local barber. Ours was above a cafe at the nearby shops. There was only one haircut our barber did for boys and that was to shear them completely! The day after you had a haircut and had to go back to junior school, you would always

A poster advertising the characters from *Planet of the Apes* coming to Plymouth Hoe in the late 1970s. They were just as good as the ones on the telly!

keep your duffle coat hood up in the playground when you arrived in case anyone laughed at you! It grew back eventually. Later on in the seventies, my mum got fed up of cutting my now longer hair so sent me into town with my friend, John, to a place called Maison Terrys to have my hair cut 'properly'. Unfortunately, on this particular Saturday, all the hairdressers were students and I got the most lopsided haircut that they could manage. They still charged the same! When we got back home, mum thought that John had cut it and that we'd kept the money; I don't remember going again after that! Boys' hair got longer and longer in the seventies. I started to grow mine longer in about 1973. The feathercut became very popular and many kids at school had their hair cut like it.

On Saturdays, Alan and I would sometimes catch the bus into town and go to the pictures. It wouldn't matter how sunny the day was (we should have been outside playing), we would still go and see the latest films. It always seemed odd coming out of the cinema in the middle of the day, emerging from the darkness into bright sunshine. One double bill I remember us going to see was *The Fantastic Journey* and *Escape From the Planet of the Apes*. I think that we left the cinema walking like apes!

On other Saturdays, we would catch the bus again and take our old records that we were fed up with to the market to see what we could get for them and then get new (second-hand) records. The dealer never gave us much in return. I remember that I'd collected all of The Monkees' albums and decided to trade them in. He gave me 50 pence! We'd also go to the second-hand bookstore where you could swap your old books for annuals and comics. We'd always come back home with something. We had a huge collection of annuals at one time and I wish that I still had them today.

As Alan got older, and we didn't hang around together much anymore, I would go to the pictures with other friends. I remember when *Planet of the Apes* was popular on TV in about 1975, a friend and I persuaded the manager of the local cinema to give us all the posters (it was my idea). They'd be worth a fortune now! Anyhow, my friend went to the cinema the day before we were meant to collect them and had the lot. I don't think we were friends for much longer.

The summer of 1976 was very hot and dry and seemed to go on forever. I still enjoyed the school holidays and was glad to be off no matter how hot it was. Nobody felt like doing much because of the heat and there were threats of standpipes. Luckily, we never got them. The local reservoir slowly dried up and Westward Television went there to do a report about it. They had just started to interview the minister involved when the heavens opened. I don't think that it stopped raining after that!

The Silver Jubilee of 1977 was a huge event. Royalty were far more popular in those days and everyone followed the Queen's visits on TV. Most streets had a street party (ours didn't), and there was a lot of flag-waving, games and plenty of food. Only recently, with the marriage of Prince William and Kate Middleton, have the streets been shut off in a similar manner all over Britain. I went to town, like thousands of other people, to see the Queen when she came to Plymouth. The film of her appearance was shown on Westward Television for years afterwards.

A selection of popular records from the 1970s. Alan and I must have ended up with loads of records, especially singles, once we started collecting them. I've still got many of the albums, but the singles all disappeared a long time ago. There was something special about getting a brand new vinyl single and playing it for the first time. I think at the time LPs were £2.99 and singles were 50 pence.

Technology changed a lot during the 1970s. When the decade started, some people still had 78rpm records and all record players came with that setting. Some had reel-to-reel tape recorders but most didn't. When cassette recorders were introduced in about 1972, every kid wanted one and most recorded their favourite pop songs on Alan Freeman's *Top 40 Show* on Sunday. We'd also try and record songs from *Top of the Pops*, but someone would always spoil it by talking. There were cartridge players as well, which were mainly used in cars, and although they lasted for a few years, they

The Queen in Armada Way, Plymouth, during the Silver Jubilee in 1977. Huge crowds turned out to see her, all waving mini Union Jack flags.

never really caught on. Digital watches were very popular for many years. People thought that it was incredible that you could push a button and the time, in digital numbers, would appear. Many ordinary dial watches were ditched or stuck in the back of a drawer as a result.

Calculators became very popular, but the kids in school seemed to use them only to spell out words such as 'Shell Oil'. Black and white TVs disappeared and were replaced by colour ones, and towards the second half of the 1970s, CB radios were introduced. CB radio, or Citizen's Band radio, was a way of communicating over short distances through a two-way radio system. It was made popular by American truck drivers and was used as their only means of communication when on the road. It was used to warn of road blocks, the police or just to chat to other truck drivers. When the single *Convoy* was released, and movies like *Smokey and the Bandit* starring Burt Reynolds and *Convoy* starring Kris Kristofferson appeared, the craze took off worldwide. People up and down the country could be seen sat in their cars saying things like 'Breaker, Breaker' or '10-4'. They all had silly names, or 'handles', for themselves like 'Rubber Duck' or 'Iceman', or something equally stupid. Our neighbour called himself 'Poodle Man' and would sit in his car for hours on end. There were various code words that were used: 'bear' meant the police; 'paper hanger' meant a policeman giving a speeding ticket; 'fender bender' meant a road accident, and so on. In those days, there were no emails, Internet or mobile phones, and Citizen's Band was a way for people to talk to each other over the airways, totally free. Sometimes it would mess up normal broadcasting so only certain channels were used.

By the time the 1970s were over, I'd left school and was no longer a kid. Music, fashion and our way of life had changed greatly over the previous ten years. I certainly missed my childhood climbing trees, building dens and being out in the sunshine all the time.

Two

SCHOOL

Our junior school wasn't very far from our house and I could leave at about five to nine in the morning, run up the bank and jump over the wall and be in the playground before the whistle blew. Once the whistle was blown we had to stay perfectly still until one of the teachers blew the whistle again and we all had to get into lines before we were led into school. The school was built into an old fort and at one end there was an open-air swimming pool. It was freezing at the best of times.

When I first started, I was put in at the tail end of the infants. We'd just come back from living in Singapore for three years and I remember the teacher introducing me to the class. We just did very basic things like a bit of reading and writing, making stuff out of plasticine, cutting shapes

I always remember the school uniform being compulsory, but looking at
my old school photo, I seem to be the only one wearing it! This photo has
December marked on the back, although it doesn't look like that time of year
in the photo. I remember every kid in this class and their names. I don't know
what happened to many of them, and I haven't seen any of them in a long
time. I'm in the front row, fifth from the left. It looks like I've just paid a visit
to the school dentist!

out of material and occasionally doing a painting which we
got to take home to our mums. I loved it and it all seemed
pretty easy. I only seemed to be in the class for a few weeks
though, until I was officially promoted to a 'junior'.

My first junior teacher was very nice and the class was
very easy going. I don't remember anyone ever getting told
off for anything.

The day started with assembly, which was taken by
the headmaster (he reminded me of a mixture of Patrick
Cargill and Rex Harrison). He seemed a very easy-going

sort of person and I can't remember him ever shouting at anyone. Assembly would start off with a hymn and then a few prayers before the headmaster gave a talk. I loved singing hymns, and the ones I remember most were *Onward Christian Soldiers*, *Kumbaya* and *Ding Dong Merrily on High*.

I remember one assembly involved the headmaster saying that kids had been spotted on the roof of the canteen building pretending to be Batman, and if anyone had any information they were to contact him. I think this sticks in my mind because one of the kids pretending to be Batman was me!

After assembly, we would be led to our classrooms. To start off with our lessons were quite basic and included spelling, early reading and writing. I've still got my school reports. I seem to have just got average marks for my schoolwork but top marks for PE and out-of-school activities. This was quite an achievement because I hated PE and never took any out-of-school activities. Even in class, I sometimes wondered if my teacher knew which one of her pupils I was!

In the morning, we'd all be given a bottle of milk and a straw. It worked out to a third of a pint. I think the milk must have come from somewhere local and there were proper milk churns kept by the canteen, which were collected daily. Sometimes bits of the farmyard could be found floating in the milk.

I seem to remember spending most of my lessons staring out of the window, imagining being Superman, watching the clock or dreaming about going home. We would have a break in the morning, one in the afternoon and about an hour and a half for dinner. Once in the playground, we would play football, marbles and conkers. Marbles and conkers seemed to be seasonal games. It's obvious why conkers would be, but not so much with marbles. I suppose it was just played when the weather was a bit warmer and drier. There was a muddy bit of ground at the end of the playground and boys would dig small pits to play their marbles. We all had a bag of marbles which we called 'alleys', and they came in various different colours. We also had larger marbles as well which were known locally as 'stumpers'. If someone's dad worked in a factory or was in the Navy, they quite often had ball bearings. The bigger they were, the more they were sought after. Both stumpers and ball bearings counted more when we were playing marbles. Some kids had it down to a fine art, but quite often I lost and would end up buying some more from the local shop. At the end of the season, which I think was just before the summer holidays, one of the bigger kids who'd won most of the marbles would shout 'scrambles' and chuck all his marbles for the other kids to try and get. We'd all run around the playground picking up as many as we could. This must have been how I got most of my marbles because I'd always end up with a big bag of them at the end of the season.

We all loved playing conkers once the autumn came. I remember spending several evenings with a friend called Colin searching for the best conker trees. We found quite a few conkers, soaking them in vinegar to make them as hard as possible. The game involved a conker on a bit of string, which you would hit off your opponent's conker. The one that didn't break or split was the winner. You would get kids saying things like, 'I've got a 29er', meaning they'd beaten twenty-nine other conker players.

At dinnertime the games were longer. Any kids who were fed up with playing football would start chanting, 'We won the War, in 1944'. It rhymed but wasn't totally accurate. As kids joined, they would put their arms around each other's shoulders until there were enough kids to play both Germans and English. Then we'd all run around the playground pretending to machine gun each other or throw pretend hand grenades! At the time, there were lots of war films on at the cinema and on the TV so we all got ideas from those. Another favourite was playing 'Cowboys and Indians'.

British Bulldog was also very popular and involved two teams which stood on either side of the playground. Kids would have to run from one side to the other while other kids in the middle tried to catch them. We also played 'it', which is also now known as 'tag'. 'Hide and seek' was also played on occasion. Of course, these were all boys' games. The girls would be busy playing hopscotch or skipping.

The class had a tuck shop, which was run by the better-behaved kids. I suppose the teachers thought that they could trust them with the money. They sold Smith's crisps, peanuts and Rich Tea biscuits. For a penny, you got eight biscuits. It doesn't sound very exciting nowadays! The peanuts came on one of those cardboard pictures of a beautiful girl and the more peanuts you bought, the more it revealed of the girl. I'm surprised that the teachers went along with this, but she always ended up having a bikini on anyway. Actually, I don't remember the last bags of peanuts ever coming off the display. Perhaps the teacher changed it for a new one to save any embarrassment!

On rainy days we would have to stay in the classroom during playtimes and read comics. The teacher would always go for a coffee break so we would generally mess around and make a lot of noise.

There was a canteen away from the school and we would all queue up there once it was midday. We were pretty well behaved as the queue went past the headmaster's office. Sometimes, we'd see one of the dinner ladies taking the headmaster his dinner on a plate. He seemed to get the same as us (poor bloke)! Meals were pretty awful from what I can remember. They were all served up with the strangest meat I've ever come across, which was very stringy with plenty of fat. Afterwards, we would have 'Jam Roly Poly', 'Spotted Dick' and 'Battered Bananas' all with custard. Some meals were edible but others most certainly weren't. Amazingly, some kids put their hands up for 'seconds' at the end of mealtimes. They obviously weren't fed at home!

I also remember that the moon landings were being shown live on TV. I think it was probably the Apollo 14 landing on 31 January 1971. Anyway, Mr Smith said that anyone who was good could go and watch it and, luckily, I was one of the kids chosen. Of course, all TV sets were black and white back then and the school set was kept in the hallway next to the assembly hall. We used to watch regular school programmes there, which I loved because it gave us a break from the mundanity of everyday lessons.

Another big thing that happened during my year in Mr Smith's class was decimalisation. Every class had charts on the wall explaining the new money, which was called 'new pence' for decades to come. Before, we had all the old coins, which were quite heavy and seemed to eventually make a hole in your pocket. I quite miss them all now, though. I always remember that school dinners were half a crown for the week, which would work out at 12½ pence nowadays. I liked all the old money and the new money seemed very small in comparison. Of course, it's all shrunk again since. I can't really remember how much pocket money I got before decimalisation, but afterwards I got 75p. I remember lots of older people complaining that they didn't understand the new money, but I don't think that it made a lot of difference to me, as all I ever bought

Apollo 14 patches were given away free with comics and I had this one sewn to my Parka coat.

was sweets. I remember that there were programmes on the radio explaining it all to us.

Probably my favourite part of our lessons was 'the programmes for schools' where we would go out into the hall and watch the school's TV. Programmes that I can remember watching, apart from the Apollo 14 moon landing, was one about an African tribe and another about pregnancy (too much for a 10-year-old).

I remember one teacher asking us what we knew about the news and the world around us. He was met with stony silence. He then asked us if we ever read the newspaper. Every kid said that the only reason they read the paper was to see what was on the telly. That was our lives back then – getting home from school, going out to play or watching all the great programmes on the TV. We had no concerns about world news, politics, the price of beans or anything else. The most we worried about was homework or if we'd forgotten our PE kit.

About twice a week we would have PE. This would take place in the assembly hall and there would be ropes set up to climb, a vaulting horse, parallel bars, footballs, balance beams and gym mats. I remember an accident that I had one day when I slipped on the balance beam. It certainly brought tears to my eyes! There was also a medicine ball that the PE teacher would throw at us. It seemed to weigh as much as I did and would take your breath away if you were struck in the wrong place. Once a week we would be taken down to the nearby fields to have a game of football. I remember on one occasion I had forgotten my kit and the PE teacher got out a box of 1950s football boots, shorts and a shirt to wear. They were about ten sizes too

A collection of pre-decimal coins, including a halfpenny, a penny, a threepence, a sixpence (the cost of a bag of chips in 1970), a one shilling piece (a 'bob'), a two shilling piece (a florin) and a half crown (my school dinner money).

big. I wondered if he did that to embarrass you so that you wouldn't forget your kit again.

The other sporting activity we enjoyed was swimming. The swimming pool was located slightly away from the school and on part of a tower, which belonged to the main part of the fort that the school occupied. In the summer, the pool was freezing, but in the winter it was even worse

PLYMOUTH EDUCATION COMMITTEE

KNOWLE PRIMARY SCHOOL, PLYMOUTH

REPORT for *Summer* .... Term, 19 *7*.

NAME *Derek Tait* .... YEAR OF JUNIOR COURSE.... *3rd.*

NUMBER IN CLASS ... *38* .... PUNCTUALITY *Satisfactory*

SUBJECTS		GRADE*	COMMENTS
ENGLISH	Reading	3	*A good reader who works quietly*
	Comprehension	4	*away at his English. He does*
	Language Study	4	*produce any thing spectacular.*
	Composition	4	*but makes steady progress.*
	Spelling	4	
ARITHMETIC 1 (Basic Skills)		4	*A little weak on tables but*
ARITHMETIC 2 (Application of skills and general Mathematics)		4	*nevertheless a sound and steady worker.*
HISTORY		4	*Not very articulate. Derek is*
GEOGRAPHY		4	*interested and progresses. Not*
SCIENCE		4	*very good under verbal questioning*
SKILLS (Craft, art, handwriting Needlework—girls)		4	*Has done some good work.*

* GRADING   Grading is done on a
seven point scale. Grade 1 represents
outstanding ability. Grade 4 is the
standard achieved by an average child.

A quiet, well behaved boy, who has worked very

PHYSICAL ACTIVITY *hard for the past year.* ..... OUT OF SCHOOL ACTIVITIES ....

HOMEWORK ....

GENERAL REMARKS *Quiet, reserved and lacking somewhat in self confidence. A well-behaved dependable boy.*

Well done - I sincerely hope his confidence will come as he is quite able.

Continued overleaf if necessary

........*D Thompson*........ Class Master/Mistress   ....*P Clear*........ Head Master

I have seen ....'s Report .... Parent's Signature
(This slip to be torn off and returned to School)

I'm amazed that I still have my school reports from Junior school. This one's about the best of them and is still pretty average. I remember that my mum laughed when she read it at the time, where it said that I was quiet because I wasn't at home! I'm impressed that I got a '4' in 'Science' as we didn't take Science, and it's good to see that when marking me in English, that the teacher has spelt 'doesn't' wrong! All kids dreaded taking their school reports home to their parents (apart from the swotty ones), but unless you were a mini Einstein (there were a couple in the class) you could expect a pretty average report every year.

and occasionally frozen over. We were still made to go in by some of the more strict, unpleasant teachers. Our aim in swimming was to get our twelve yards certificate and then our twenty-five yards certificate. Once you managed to swim twenty-five yards, the headmaster would award you a certificate at the next assembly meeting. You also got a patch with an 'S' (for swimmer) to sew on your swimming costume. I think that our parents had to pay 5s for these. In the summer holidays, the pool would be open to local residents who would pay 1s to swim.

I remember that there was a school dentist who really was appalling. He'd drill your teeth and it would hurt like mad. He reminded me of the character Laurence Olivier played in *The Marathon Man*. One kid at school said that when he went to his family dentist, the dentist gave him an injection to numb the pain before he did any drilling. We didn't believe him because we were all used to the terrible school dentist who didn't seem to care one way or the other. Perhaps he was saving money. Back in the 1970s, they would give you gas if they were going to pull out any teeth. Having gas was awful and, although you didn't feel anything, it wasn't much fun and left you feeling groggy afterwards. The school also had an optician who would come around and check your eyesight and make sure that you weren't colour blind. Some kids had lazy eyes and had to wear wire-rimmed NHS glasses with a pink Elastoplast over one of the lenses. There was also a nit nurse who would come around every so often and examine the tops of our heads.

As I moved up the classes, the teachers became stricter and I can't remember the lessons being as much fun. I do remember one teacher whose lessons consisted of what he'd read in *The Sun* that morning and what he did during the war. Oh, and his boring holiday slides! He once told us – because he'd read it in the paper – that budgies had no brains. We all had budgies back in the 1970s and this seemed very hard to believe, but you couldn't disagree with him or else he would go off on one. People's knowledge in the 1970s, even teachers', wasn't like it is today, and anything written in a newspaper or book, no matter how far-fetched, was taken as fact. Our teacher had lots of these curious facts, many of which I now realise were complete rubbish. I wish that I could remember more of them.

In the Easter, summer and Christmas holidays, the school had a fete and the admission was 1s. We were all given tickets to sell and we'd make sure that our parents and neighbours bought some. I think that there was a prize for the person who sold the most. I recall that Mr Smith had set up one of those metal hoops that you had to navigate along a piece of wire without it touching the sides and making a buzzing noise. This seemed very hi-tech to us in those days and I could never do it.

The fete also included a raffle and a jumble sale. I remember coming away with some comics and a couple of squeaky toys for my dog, Shep. Alan won all sorts, mainly bottles of wine (he was only 14 but no one was bothered in those days) on the spin-the-wheel competition. The wheel was about 4ft high and a teacher would spin it, and if you picked the number it fell on, you won a prize. I was amazed that Alan won so much and it wasn't until much later that I realised that the wheel was mis-shapen and tended to stop on the number opposite to the one it started on. Perhaps that's why Alan got Grade One Maths and I didn't!

There seemed to be lots of police officers around back then. There was always a constable on the beat and I remember a girl at junior school winning a prize because she had 'looked right, looked left and then looked right again' before crossing the road. I recall the policeman coming to school and awarding her the prize in assembly. This impressed me and every time I saw a policeman I looked right, left and right again. It never got me anywhere and I never won anything.

All the kids collected bubblegum cards, which we would swap in the playground. In junior school it was mostly football cards, but later on I remember everyone collecting cards from *Kung Fu, The Six Million Dollar Man, Planet of the Apes* and *Kojak*. We also collected a lot of badges that came free with ice cream, sweets, cereal and from shops.

Every Friday we'd have an end of the day assembly and we'd always sing the same hymn, *Now the Day is Over*. I've never heard it since. Once assembly was over, we'd all run to get outside as fast as possible. We were always told off for running in the corridor, but your punishment depended on who caught you. The stricter teachers would either give you the cane, lines or detention. The nicer teachers would just tell you to 'stop running!'

There was a period after passing my eleven-plus when I was still at junior school, before we broke up for the summer holidays and before we went to our new schools. Because only seven of us had passed the eleven-plus, the teacher decided to make me a prefect. I hated that. I didn't want to be standing in the corridor telling kids off for running,

A collection of bubblegum cards that we all loved to collect at school.

I wanted to be out in the playground messing around. We also had to sit on chairs and watch the assembly and tell kids off who were talking. It was embarrassing even then and, of course, I never told anyone off. Once a week, if you were a prefect, you had to go to one of the staff rooms with the other prefects to have a talk with the local vicar. I think the talk was about forty minutes long and he discussed God and Jesus etc. Seems odd now. Anyway, I never minded because it got me out of class for a while.

Violence in the classroom towards kids back then seemed to be almost acceptable. There was the cane, of course, and

I remember that the deputy head would rap you across the hand with it if you weren't working quickly enough. He also liked to bang his knuckles off your head. I found him to be very strict and didn't like him at all, but some kids seemed to take to him. Looking back, I suppose he did have his good points and wasn't as bad as some of the teachers that taught me later.

By 1972, I was off to the nearby comprehensive school. Many of the friends I'd made at junior school still had another year there. Since I was born in August, I seemed to be bumped up a year. One of my friends in class was only ten days younger than me and not only had to do another year at junior school, but also had to do another year at the comprehensive.

It was the first time I really had to get a bus on my own. Luckily, Alan went to the same school. I think that the bus broke down on the very first day and we had to walk the rest of the way. It's hard to imagine now that the busy road the bus used to travel along was then unmade and was just rocks, earth and gravel. When we got to school, we had to meet up in the main assembly hall and were given a talk before we lined up to go to our new tutorials. For the first time we had to wear proper uniforms – a blazer, school tie, white shirt and dark trousers. There was one item of clothing that we all disliked wearing. The boys had to wear school caps, even off the premises, and the girls had to wear straw boaters. You could get lines, detention or even the cane if you were caught not wearing them. We also had to wear blue coats; no other colour was allowed. I was the first kid to wear a blue Parka but soon everyone had them. We had to hang our coats in the cloakroom, which meant that everyone's coat looked the same and someone would invariably take yours home.

On our first day, once we were in our tutorials, we were issued with bus passes and our timetables. I can't really remember much about what we did the first day. I think that we were just shown around the school. The sixth formers were put in charge of us and were very friendly. I remember after school telling my mum that they were just like adults and one even had a moustache! Of course, in reality, he was only 16 and it wasn't actually much of a moustache …

We now had a whole range of lessons to deal with which included Geography, History, Religious Education, German, English, Maths, Art, Craftwork, Biology and Chemistry. I think, apart from English, I hated them all. Games and PE were no fun whatsoever. I'm sure that some kids enjoyed it but some of the teachers left a lot to be desired. On Friday mornings we would have our art lesson, which I would have enjoyed if it weren't for the double period of Games straight afterwards. Games to me were something that you played out of school and were about enjoying yourself. Being constantly shouted at, being made to run outside in shorts and t-shirts when there was three inches of snow on the ground or forced to run miles during cross-country was no fun to me at all. We could wear tracksuits when it was cold, but again they had to be dark blue. If you had a green, grey or red tracksuit, you were shouted at and not allowed to wear it.

We didn't see our PE teacher much because he was often topping up his tan on his sun lounger. I remember the same teacher giving a group of boys the cane because they had crossed the road during cross-country. How unfair

The pendant that I made for my mum in our first year Craftwork class. Amazingly, she has kept it all these years. I can't imagine that she ever wore it though.

was that? Surely crossing the road was an easy task for an 11-year-old to accomplish and shouldn't have been questioned. There were lots of punishments in the seventies for really minor things which teachers nowadays would not get away with.

Every morning we'd have tutorial before we started our main lessons. We were all split up into 'houses' of different colours. Each house had its own assembly and, in the summer, would compete against each other during Sports Day.

We all had to cover our exercise books, for some unknown reason, which meant that many kids had books with offcuts of the latest crazy, fashionable seventies wallpaper designs. There were certainly some unusual ones. It was just as well we did have to cover our books because I would draw cartoons all over mine, much to the annoyance of the stricter teachers. There were no lockers in those days so all your books had to be carried around with you all day long. The coolest thing to have back then was an Adidas bag, the bigger the better. I reckon that you could have fitted a dead body in most of them they were so big, and even then there wasn't enough room for all your books, pens, packed lunch, sports kit, football boots, etc.

The fashion was to get the biggest knot in your school tie that you possibly could, which made the length of the tie only about 4 inches long. Boys competed to have the biggest flares (we'd measure them), the tallest platforms and the widest collars.

We had used pencils at junior school but now we had to use ink pens or fountain pens. Biros were invented but heaven help the boy who dared to use one. All fountain pens leaked and were absolutely useless. Every kid went home with a black hand due to his leaking pen; some had inky top pockets (much to their mum's chagrin), and the stranger kids had black tongues from where they had sucked their pens all day.

Lessons were long and boring. Sometimes we would have quadruple Maths, which meant it went on all morning. Half an hour of Maths (especially with our teachers) was bad enough, but three hours was hellish. Physics and Chemistry were also long and tedious. At least with Geography and History we got taken out occasionally. I remember one Geography lesson when we got to spend the morning exploring the nearby woods.

Sometimes, we would be shown a film in the afternoon. There were no TV projectors or DVDs back then so one of the teachers would have to load the film manually onto a film projector. The films normally came in three reels, which meant that there was some interruption halfway through when one of the reels came to an end.

The films would always be shown in the 'music room'. The music room was so called because it had a few musical instruments in it that had all seen better days. The only film that I can remember being treated to was Charles Dickens' *Great Expectations*, which was the old black and white version starring John Mills. It was good to just get the afternoon off lessons, even if the film wasn't the latest James Bond! The hard plastic chairs that we had to sit on for two hours soon became very uncomfortable …

As the school had its own projector (although perhaps it belonged to one of the teachers), they occasionally showed films after school. I think the religious teacher might have organised this because one film featured Johnny Cash singing gospel songs and another was called *The Cross and the Switchblade*, which starred Pat Boone. I loved Johnny Cash but didn't go to see either film. The only one that I remember staying behind to see was *It's Only Money* starring Jerry Lewis. Kids loved Jerry Lewis back in the 1970s, and acts like Laurel and Hardy and Abbot and Costello were also incredibly popular.

All the teachers had nicknames, often from the cartoons and TV programmes of the day. One was called 'Orinoco' after the character in *The Wombles* (he had a big nose), and the headmaster was known as 'Basil'. I'm not sure why this was, as it certainly wasn't after the character in *Fawlty Towers*.

The fashions that we all remember from the 1970s were just coming in and I remember that platform shoes were only allowed to be a certain size (teachers would measure them), hair could only come an inch below the collar and in no circumstances were white socks to be worn. I think it was when I started going to the comprehensive that I realised that many teachers didn't seem to like kids at all (especially the PE teachers), and many of them appeared to us to be quite unbalanced.

Other lessons included Computer Studies, despite the fact that the school only had one computer, which back in the 1970s didn't do much (if anything). The school also had a language laboratory. There was absolutely no point to this at all, although it was thought to be very modern. The whole class would sit in cubicles with headphones on and the teacher would ask them a question in French, Spanish or German. Even when I was 11, I realised that this could all have been achieved in an ordinary classroom without the expense of a language lab.

Contact lenses must have become popular in the 1970s because I remember that a couple of the male teachers suddenly no longer needed to wear glasses. Our Maths teacher always held his hands like James Cagney when he was talking and, with his new contact lenses in, his face was all screwed up and his eyes watered profusely. When he turned his back, we'd all say, 'You dirty rat!' in our best James Cagney voices. *Who Do You Do?* was on the telly at the time so everybody tried his or her hand at impressions. Most were of Bruce Forsyth or John Inman and most weren't very good. Saying 'I'm Free!' to a teacher in your squeakiest voice didn't seem to go down too well. Anyhow, we all had a laugh at the Maths teacher's expense. Another vain teacher lost his contact lens on the football pitch and had everyone down on their hands and knees searching for it. Amazingly, one pupil managed to find it.

Occasionally, lessons were interesting. I remember one lesson when our Chemistry teacher set fire to himself. Fortunately, he was very quickly put out and didn't suffer any ill effects!

The school had one modern appliance – the drinks machine. They're commonplace nowadays but back then it was unheard of for a school to have one. From what I can remember it dispensed hot chocolate, coffee, tea and

Calculators and digital watches came out at around this time. They were about £175 when they first appeared, but were reduced in price later on. The more studious kids seemed to have their own calculators, although the Maths teachers frowned upon them and made sure we all used our slide rules instead.

hot blackcurrant. It was very popular with all the kids, but then one day one of the stricter teachers decided that the discarded cups were creating a bit of a mess and pulled the plug. Of course, she didn't care. She could go back to her nice warm staffroom with its electric kettle.

There seemed to be a lot of sport at the school, including football, cricket, rounders, rugby and basketball. We all loved basketball at the time because of the Harlem Globetrotters. Most of us just knew them from the cartoon on the TV. We also had cross-country. Every school at the time had a PE teacher who was a bully and ours was no different. It was no fun getting your ear or hair pulled, or having inane comments shouted in your lugholes.

Teachers were a different breed back in the 1970s. You seemed to be able to get the cane for just about anything, but the main crime seemed to be 'mitching' or playing truant. In class, chalk regularly flew past your head if you were talking. Even then, the teachers realised that this was wrong and I remember one kid getting a piece of chalk right in his eye. There were teachers that you knew not to mess with and others that you would spend the whole lesson taking the mickey out of. Student teachers were the best to have fun with, and no matter what they did they never came out on top.

At break times, most of us just met up in the playground. If you didn't like football, then there wasn't much else to do. Occasionally, there would be a game of British Bulldog in the bottom playground, but the games we all loved like marbles and conkers seemed to be things of the past.

School dinnertimes weren't much better. The meals were on a par with my previous school, and then some bright spark on the teaching staff decided to introduce packed lunches, so we all ended up bringing our own sandwiches. I think that school dinners were about 15 pence a day. Even after you'd eaten your dinner, there was still about an hour to kill, so many kids headed up to the nearby shopping centre. Most kids would go to the bakery at the shopping square and either buy a pasty or chips, or things called an 'elephant's foot', which was like a big chocolate eclair filled with cream. Everyone loved them.

There was a cinema club on Fridays where you could watch the latest film that the Art teacher had managed to get his hands on. The projector occasionally broke down and the only film I can remember seeing all the way through was one about The Beatles.

The school also had a library and, at the front, a small putting green. Crazy golf was very popular in the 1970s.

Every year the school would have a mufti day. Tickets for it were 5 pence and, once you bought one, you could wear whatever you liked to school. During the glam rock days, all the boys turned up in their biggest flares, loudest shirts and tightest tank tops. I think that the teachers joined in, but with a lot of them it was hard to tell if they were wearing mufti or not.

In around 1975, *Doctor Who* was very popular and Tom Baker had taken over the role. Another kid and I decided to build a Dalek. The plans were in a *Radio Times* special, and the whole project was quoted as costing £12. It all looked pretty straightforward. Every dinnertime we would travel up to the shops and go to a DIY store to buy something that might come in handy for our Dalek construction. Of course, we never got very far and the project was soon abandoned.

Years later I finally built a Dalek, which lived in my cellar and occasionally in the garden. Like most Daleks, it ended up on eBay.

The summer of 1976, and leading up to it, was incredibly hot and dry. One teacher decided to let us do our lessons outside where it was cooler. However, she was called into the headmaster's office and told off, and we were soon back in a sticky, humid classroom.

The bus journeys to and from school were an experience all of their own. Luckily, the school had its own buses specially laid on because I don't think any 'civilians' getting on our bus would have enjoyed the journey very much. The trip going to school was never too rowdy. The bus always had a driver and a conductor who would let you stand at the front of the bus if you wanted to. Some kids would get rolls of bus tickets from the drivers that would later be

PREFECT

In my final year, I was press-ganged into being a prefect. Things weren't all bad, though; I had to do my prefect duty with an ex-Miss Westward. Even then, I don't think I turned up all of the time.

thrown around the playground. Most kids would have bus passes, which we had to show to the conductor, but others would have to pay. You could only get a bus pass if you lived further than three miles from the school. I got a bus pass, but a boy living just a few houses away didn't. I used to smuggle my bus pass to him under the seat until the conductor caught us and confiscated it. He soon gave it back, though, when I was getting off. Whereas the trip to school was relatively calm, the one returning home was bedlam. The kids would be screaming and shouting and generally causing havoc, swinging from the bars and jumping on the seats. The driver and the conductors couldn't do much to control it so didn't bother most of the time. But it was all pretty harmless fun.

Our exams were all taken in the Games Hall – rows and rows of pupils all taking their O Levels and CSEs. It was pretty hard to concentrate.

By the time I left school in the late 1970s, things had changed vastly over the decade. I was asked by the careers teacher to stay on as a lab assistant in the Chemistry room, but I turned it down and left as soon as I could. That evening, I made sure that I cleared out all of my schoolbooks and put them straight out for the rubbish. When *Grange Hill* was shown on TV in the late 1970s, I realised that all schools had the same ingredients, which included the strict deputy headmaster, the unconfident supply teacher and the bully-boy PE instructor!

Three

FRIENDS

I seemed to know John from the time I started at juniors to well after I left school altogether. I can't remember how we met but we were always in the same class. His mum worked at the Magnet Restaurant in town where we went as a family every Saturday. I seem to remember eating a lot of oxtail soup there!

John and I went everywhere. We'd catch buses out to Dartmoor or around Plymouth Hoe, or to places we'd never heard of. We went fishing in the creek (we never caught anything), collected tadpoles, searched for bats, looked for flying saucers (when *UFO* was on the TV), played crazy golf, went to the cinema and generally explored.

After Scouts, we would always go to the local fish and chip shop and get a bag of chips, which were sixpence

(2½p), and then have a wander around until we had to go home. I suppose we were about 9 or 10 years old.

I used to go into those passport machines that were in the bus station many times with friends. Alan and I had some great photos but they've all got lost over the years. In those days it was about 20p to have four photos taken.

John and I decided to make some money one summer holiday by washing people's cars. We worked out all the hundreds of pounds that we would make, but in the end nobody was interested. We even bought our own bucket and sponge.

David lived in the flats nearby and briefly came to our junior school. It seemed he was there one year but was gone the next. This seemed to happen often and nobody ever appeared to know where all these kids disappeared to. For a year we were great friends. I remember that he was one of the first kids to get a Raleigh chopper bike. They were incredibly expensive in those days (£36) and most parents couldn't afford them. David's bike was blue and he let me ride it around the nearby football pitch. In the evening, he would call for me and we'd play commandos in the piles of earth that had been deposited at the end of the street. He always wore a green parka coat and before he came out, he would fill the pockets up with Golden Nuggets so that we had something to eat.

His mum used to make us dinner in their flat on the 7th floor, and then we would go out playing in the nearby woods, running through old drains. We used to head down to a nearby village and buy gobstoppers in the little shop there. One week, his mum took us both to the ABC to see the James Bond film *Diamonds are Forever*. I was meant to be at the Scouts, and as we rode on the double-decker bus into town, two of the other Scouts in the group saw me and waved as if to say I was going the wrong way. Going to see James Bond was much more fun. David and I were always swapping things like soldiers, comics and other toys. I've still got his 1971 Esso FA Cup medals. I remember swapping the Rolykin Daleks with him that I brought back from Butlins and then finding out that he'd smashed them to get the ball bearings out. Ball bearings were prized in games of marbles.

I was also good friends with a kid called Colin. He was in my class and he and David knew each other, but didn't seem to get on. In the evening, Colin and I would go looking for conkers. One day, when both David and Colin came to call for me, I remember my mum had bought a rocking chair and I had the box in my room to play in. It seemed huge to me and I kept it for ages. It was many things – a boat, a car or a spaceship. When David and Colin came, we all just piled into it. You wouldn't think three kids would fit in a box, but we did. In the end, we were making so much noise enjoying ourselves that mum told us off and we went outside to play.

Colin lived with his gran and I would visit him at weekends. I remember us playing with bows and arrows in his gran's garden. One evening, we had been collecting conkers when a gang of kids set on us as we were cutting through some school grounds to get back home. One older kid punched me and I had a bleeding nose. When we got back to Colin's gran's house, she just told me off for fighting!

Colin was a lovely kid and I remember that he would save his Space slides for me that came free with Sugar Puffs. I had a camera and a slide projector back then, but unfortunately film was very expensive and most of the photos I have are of my best friend, my dog Shep.

When I started comprehensive school in 1972, I soon made friends with a kid called Nicholas Rich. The first time I saw him, he was having a fight with someone. Nick was the kind of kid that was always in trouble. He loved playing practical jokes, and although they had me in stitches, they didn't always go down too well with the teachers. He must have kept the local joke shop, Jack Cohens, in business as he always had itching powder, stink bombs, inky soap, and things like that.

In the summer of 1973, Nick and I hung around together visiting the zoo, catching buses wherever they went and exploring the old air-raid shelters on Dartmoor. We would go into town or Nick would come round my house with his Action Men and we'd dangle them out the window.

I remember that Uri Geller was on the TV a lot in the early 1970s and we were in the canteen once when the deputy headmaster appeared, yelling: 'Which boy did this?' He held up a fork that was bent in half. Many of us laughed – we had all been trying to bend spoons with our minds after seeing Uri on TV.

We had a Chemistry lesson one day where the teacher showed us how to nickel plate copper items. Nick nickel-plated all the 2p pieces that he had in his pocket and passed them off as 10p pieces at the local sweet shop later that day. When I first saw *Grange Hill* later on in the 1970s, it seemed to me that it was just how things were in those days.

Four

CARS, BUSES AND PETROL

The 1970s, to me, had some of the best cars. They might have been unreliable rust buckets but they certainly seemed to have plenty of character. The photograph on p. 58 shows my dad cleaning our Vauxhall Viva in about 1971. It was a bonus if it got to the end of the street as it was forever breaking down. There were a lot fewer cars in the street in those days and it was unusual to see any passing traffic. Our immediate neighbours had an Austin Maxi. We travelled all over the place in the Viva, but even though there were less cars on the road it seemed slow going getting to the beach in the summer, probably because the roads were narrower and more congested. Dad would take his car whenever he had a posting with the Navy in the UK, so mum, Alan and I would always catch the local

Dad with our Vauxhall Viva.

double-decker bus into town to go shopping or to go to the pictures.

I know that the Viva was always breaking down, but I don't remember ever getting stuck anywhere in it. It must have been the Viva that we took all the way to Butlins in Clacton when we went in 1970. Altogether, we had three cars in the seventies – the Viva and two Hillman Avengers. I remember when the Avenger came out. It seemed very posh then. The advert showed them being offloaded from a plane with the theme from the 1960s TV show *The Avengers* playing in the background.

When I was a kid, there were certainly plenty of Fords about, including the Cortina, the Escort and the Capri. Blue Ford Escorts seemed to be everywhere and must have been one of the most popular cars of the day.

I only remember some of the cars in the street. Perhaps most people didn't have them. One I remember was a Vauxhall Victor, which was like a large Viva, and a few houses along, in about 1975, someone bought a Princess which seemed very flash and modern back then. The only other car in the street that sticks in my mind was a white Lotus sports car, which reminded me of the car belonging to *The Saint* or *The Persuaders*. It was very unusual to know someone who owned a sports car back in the 1970s. Nowadays, they're everywhere.

Green Shield Stamps were very popular at one time and the garages would offer you double stamps if you bought your petrol there. Eventually, as the garages tried to compete, they would offer you more and more stamps, with some offering twelve times the amount you would normally get. There was a Green Shield Stamp shop in the town

A busy car park in the city centre of Plymouth. Every make of car that
was popular at the time can be seen. The building on the right is the ABC
Cinema and, when a popular movie was shown, queues used to stretch right
back around the wall that can be seen by Derry's Clock.

and the stamps, once stuck in booklets, could be redeemed
for gifts of the day, which included things like clock radios,
Teasmades, etc. The two things that I remember us getting
from the Green Shield Stamp shop was an electric mower
(very modern then) and a garden gnome. He's still around
somewhere.

We certainly travelled far and wide in our Viva, and
wherever you went in those days, it quite often seemed like
you had the place to yourself. Even driving into town, there
were quiet days when there was hardly anyone else shopping. It's certainly different today.

The police had their own little cars. Nowadays, they seem
to have top-of-the-range cars, but back then they had little

Austin 1100s and later Ford Escorts. There were many other models of police cars, but most at the time seemed to be Austins or Fords.

Another favourite vehicle from the 1970s was the ice-cream van. The van would turn up on every street and there would be a queue of kids waiting to be served. You knew when it was coming by the music it played. The tunes I can remember were *Greensleeves*, *Popeye the Sailorman* and *Raindrops Keep Falling on my Head*. I'm sure there were others and there were various other tunes up and down the country.

Some are still played today.

This booklet is still full of Green Shield Stamps. The store must have shut down before my mum had time to use them. Everybody used to collect them, and stamps were given away with purchases everywhere.

Five

HOLIDAYS

I loved the school holidays and always counted the days until the next ones. I remember our holiday in 1970 because we went to Butlins at Clacton. Everyone went to Butlins back then for their holidays and it was very unusual to hear of anyone travelling abroad. I remember we were hoping to go to Butlins at Minehead but it was booked up, so we went to Clacton instead which was quite a drive. There were endless funfair rides, all free, including dodgems, a big wheel and a big dipper. The only drawback was that you had to queue for quite a while to get a go. We spent a lot of the time in the arcades and, apart from the slot machines, our favourite attraction was the crane grab machine. The machines were always filled with impossible-to-get watches and other luxury items, but we managed to get lots of Rolykin Daleks. Alan and I both loved *Doctor Who* at the time (which then starred Patrick Troughton) so we were happy to win them. Nowadays, the same Daleks sell on eBay for anything up to £100 each.

There was a booth that you could go in at Butlins, which would record your voice and play it back to you. This fascinated many kids. We made friends with a boy from Manchester who seemed to spend a lot of time saying rude things to the machine just so he could hear them played back. This was before cassette players came onto the market.

I remember going on the boating lake with Alan and him jumping out of the boat and pushing me back into the middle without a paddle. We also went roller-skating and generally enjoyed wandering around the site. The chalets weren't up to much but as kids we didn't notice. A bird had made a nest just outside our chalet, which seemed wonderful back then and we would check every day to see if the eggs had hatched.

We never went as a family again to Butlins but had other holidays later at Pontins.

Most summers, in the early 1970s, were spent exploring the nearby woods and building dens. I read Enid Blyton's *Secret Seven* books at the time, so I imagined everyone we came across was up to no good. Michael, who lived along the street, and I saw two men stuffing the pigs that lived in the woods into the back of a truck. The poor things didn't have an inch to move and, thinking about it now, they were probably off to market. Our imaginations ran wild and we thought the men had turned up to steal them.

Reading Enid Blyton stories fuelled a lot of my early adventures, and I really believed that my friends and I could come across lost treasure while out or foil some criminal's activities and save the day by contacting the police. TV shows like *The Flaxton Boys* stoked our imaginations, and there were many other programmes that made life for a young boy seem like one long adventure.

We would go to the beach quite often. Once it was the summer holidays the roads would be congested and packed with holidaymakers. There certainly seemed to be a lot more caravans back then. The main road into Cornwall went over the Tamar Bridge, which was a toll road, and collecting the money led to huge tailbacks. It would seem a long, hot, sticky journey getting anywhere, and we were always relieved to arrive at our destination. Once there, the car park and the beach would be packed and we'd find our own patch and throw down a towel. Mum always took a picnic and a thermos flask. I was never a very good swimmer, although Alan was. We would always take the lilo and I'd float around on that. I remember everyone had them and there was an advert on the TV warning people not to go out of their depth while lying on them and to stay in sight of their parents.

At the beginning of the 1970s, the first surfboards appeared on the beaches in England. As far as I can remember they were all made of polystyrene. They were very similar to the paddles that we were given at school when we were learning to swim. Most of my day at the beach would involve searching rock pools and pestering mum and dad to get me an ice cream or a lolly. We always had a great time. One year we hired a caravan, which was right beside the beach. It was quite old as it still had gas lamps. Alan and I would wander to the nearby arcade near the

This photo shows me at the beach searching rock pools for small fish and shrimps. Note the patches on my trousers. Patches were fashionable at the time, which was handy because I was always putting the knees out of my trousers. I remember that the patch on one knee was of Wile E. Coyote, and I had another one of Bugs Bunny on my pocket. The other knee had sergeant's stripes!

next beach and play on the fruit machines and go on the dodgems that they had there. I remember that it rained for most of the holiday and we eventually came home early.

Back home there was a pond near the woods and in the holidays I would go searching for tadpoles. I'd always find some and my dream was to have a full-sized frog just like the one Catweazle had on television. I would take the tadpoles home and keep them in a jam jar on the window ledge. Eventually, they would start to grow legs and, if we were lucky, they would turn into tiny frogs. My tadpole days came to an end when we were set upon and beaten up by some older teenagers. I was about 10 at the time and they were about 15. Not only did they beat me up, they also stamped on my tadpoles! In those days, nobody called the police when kids got into a fight, but I told my brother about it all and he went looking for them. Of course, they were long gone.

Another thing we would do in the summer holidays was to collect butterflies. Many kids had butterfly nets and there were certainly a lot more butterflies in the 1970s and many, many different varieties. I always made sure that I let them go, unharmed, afterwards. There seemed to be something in boys that made them want to collect things, and many had collections of birds' eggs, which were taken from nests, had a pin put in one end so that the insides could be blown out and were then put on display. Again, I didn't want to do anything like this so the only eggs I had were bits of shell left by birds who had long since hatched and flown away.

I remember one summer in the early 1970s when there were ladybirds absolutely everywhere. Nowadays, it's amazing if you see one, but in that summer there were millions.

I collected some in a matchbox and took them to show a friend who lived in the nearby block of flats. We let them all go later.

Mum took me to Blackpool one year on a coach and I recall it took forever to get there. We were booked into a bed and breakfast, which like a lot of them wasn't up to much. While we were there it rained most of the time. I think that we went on the trams one night and in the day-time we went to Madame Tussauds and Ripley's 'Believe It or Not' museum. Some of the exhibits in Madame Tussauds, although made of wax, were pretty gory. I certainly never wanted to go again. Their toyshops had toys that you couldn't get in Plymouth and I came home with a Red Indian Mohican figure. I also remember visiting a lot of the penny arcades while we were there.

Every Easter and summer, Whitleggs Fair would come to town and set up base at Central Park. I would hassle mum and dad to take me and we would go in the evenings. I loved the dodgems most of all, but there were many other rides like the Cyclone and the Waltzer that always made everyone feel a bit sick. There were also rifle ranges and hoopla games. Occasionally, I think that we even won something. It was usually a cuddly toy or something similar. There were many slot machines as well, which in the early 1970s still took the old pennies. In the holidays, Alan and I would get our pocket money and walk to Central Park to get to the fair. It was about two miles away, but we didn't want to waste any money on the bus fare. We always came back home with nothing, but if we did have a bit of change we would buy sweets from one of the many shops on the way back.

A day out with Shep on Dartmoor. I'm wearing my favourite Parka coat covered in various military patches. Shep looks like he's just noticed the local wildlife.

Every so often the fair would be set up closer to home and we would wander up to the field behind us in Whitleigh. Amazingly, one year the fair was set up just at the end of our street. There was a patch of bare land there and as far as I can remember it was the only time it happened.

The latest pop music was played constantly, especially on the dodgems. I remember whizzing around to Alvin Stardust's *Coo Ca Choo* and Sweet's *Blockbuster*. Certain songs always remind me of the fair. *Seasons in the Sun* by Terry Jacks always reminds me of walking to Central Park to the fair because it was played continually. Other memories of the fair include eating giant hotdogs and lots of candyfloss. The fair had its own noise and smell. It was a

In about 1971 we all went to Bristol Zoo and this photo shows some of
the fashions of the day. I'm wearing my favourite cords (they made a noise
when I walked), and mum is wearing a trouser suit. The girl on the left of the
picture was the trendiest of all of us.

mixture of all the rides, the hot food and people. Sometimes
you would get rough kids who would start fights or jump
in your dodgem and ruin things, but it didn't seem to
happen often. I remember getting told off a lot for driving
the wrong way and bumping people – we always tried to
bump the girls.

Every summer, the Radio One Roadshow would come
to Plymouth Hoe and we'd always try to go. It used to get
absolutely packed. I think in separate years we saw Kid
Jensen, Dave Lee Travis and, best of all, Tony Blackburn.
The DJs would get people up on stage who would have
a chance to win records and other stuff. There were lots of

live bands, too. We used to listen to Radio One all the time (we even took transistors with earphones into classes at school), and we would follow the route of the Roadshow around the country and look forward to it coming to Plymouth.

There weren't many radio stations when I was a boy, just the BBC ones and Radio Luxembourg. I'd listen to Luxembourg late at night, but the sound would be constantly disappearing and it was very hard to hear your favourite tunes. Even so, all the kids at school listened to it. Plymouth got its own radio station in 1975 and I went to the opening event at the Guildhall in the hope of getting some free records. Regrettably, I came away empty-handed. There were lots of competitions on the radio, and if you

The 'Hairy Cornflake', Dave Lee Travis, hosting the Radio One Roadshow on Plymouth Hoe in 1978.

phoned in you could win some singles. All the kids at school did this, but the singles you won were always appalling and recorded by acts you'd never heard of.

I remember one holiday when Alan and I explored the nearby woods; he climbed up onto one of the many forts in the area and looked through the window. He said that it was full of guns and he could hear voices coming from inside. This seemed very 'Secret Seven' to me, and it was decided that we'd save up for a rope so that I could also climb up and see. By the time I'd saved up my pocket money and bought a rope from the local Make and Mend shop, Alan had discovered girls and that was the end to our summer-time adventures!

I loved the half-term holiday, which near enough tied in with Guy Fawkes Night. The week before the event, all the kids would make a guy and sit on street corners shouting, 'Penny for the Guy!' Many people would give you a penny, which was worth a lot more then, but on occasion someone more generous would give you a 2s piece.

When bonfire night came around, everyone would join in and all the kids would have sparklers while the parents roasted potatoes and chestnuts (which had been collected earlier from the woods). We would then have firework displays in each other's back garden. The fire-works weren't as impressive as they are now, just a few rockets, Catherine Wheels and other assorted fireworks with names like Spitfire, Flying Saucer, Retro-Jet, Jackpot and Harlequin. Some kids would throw bangers around the street, and every year there were adverts on TV about the dangers of them. Blue Peter and Magpie would warn you to check your bonfire in case there were hedgehogs

This photo shows me at Longleat in about 1975. I wasn't looking at the girl in the mini-skirt – honest! We went to see the lions (most were asleep), but my favourite parts of the park were the monkeys, who happily dismantled every car, and the Doctor Who Exhibition, which contained my favourite of Doctor Who's enemies – the Daleks. I came home with lots of souvenirs from the exhibition, including photos and badges.

living in it. Despite all the unsupervised bonfires that went on, I can't recall anyone ever getting injured. At the end of the night, we'd all go home smelling of smoke. When we closed our eyes, it still seemed possible to see all the flames and fireworks.

I loved the Christmas holidays and the anticipation of all the presents that we had coming. The lead-up to Christmas was just as exciting. We would open an advent calendar door every morning to reveal which day of December it was. Each depicted a biblical scene behind it or something to do with Christmas. It doesn't seem very exciting now, but we loved it at the time and it was all part of the Christmas fun. At junior school, we'd have the Christmas fete, Nativity play and Christmas party. All I can remember about the party was lots of jelly, making paper chains and decorating the classroom.

Alan and I would often go carol singing. All the kids did it in those days. Sometimes, for a laugh, Alan would knock on the door and then run off and hide behind a hedge leaving me singing on my own. We always made a few pennies out of it and enjoyed it at the time.

At home, mum would put up all the decorations and the Christmas tree. When I was about 8, my mum, dad and Alan would try to convince me that there actually was a Santa. They would leave out biscuits and milk for the reindeers and, when we still slept in bunk beds, Alan convinced me that we could hear Santa's sleigh bells. Maybe it was just the early signs of tinnitus! I always fell asleep long before my mum and dad entered the room and left our presents.

We always woke up early on Christmas morning and opened our presents, before jumping on mum and dad's bed at 7 a.m. We got some great presents, including lots of annuals, my favourites being *The Beano* and *The Dandy*. I remember one year when we got a table football game with handles either side to flick the ball into the goal. That was in 1970. It was just like the one we had played on at Butlins.

When we grudgingly returned to junior school after the holidays, we always had to write an essay entitled, 'What I did on my school holiday'. Some things we couldn't write about because they would have been frowned upon by the teacher – I'm sure they never quite realised how much fun we all had.

I would love to read those old essays today and relive all those happy days we had outdoors playing in the sun. I wonder if some of them still exist somewhere in an old school cupboard or if they were thrown away a long time ago. I think that I already know the answer.

Six

ACTIVITIES

Many boys either belonged to the Cubs or Scouts and the girls belonged to the Brownies or the Guides. My friend John had persuaded me to join the Scouts so we went along to the nearest Scout hut and enrolled. It must have been in winter time because I remember the evenings being dark. I also remember the year – 1971. Mum wouldn't buy me the uniform because she knew, quite rightly, that I would probably get fed up with it. Kids' mums would buy their uniforms in stages starting with the woggle and neckerchief. I didn't even get that far. We used to go every Thursday or Friday evening, and my memories include learning the pledges to Queen and country.

On Saturday, we had to go there early in the morning and we would learn how to use a compass and do a bit of map reading. Back then it made no sense to me what-soever. I think I stayed in the Scouts for about six weeks before realising that I'd rather lie in on Saturday mornings. Alan had been on a school trip to Holland and brought me back a Scout knife as a present. Lots of kids carried penknives in those days, not for any violent use but just because it's what every kid had. The Swiss Army knives had attachments like screwdrivers, corkscrews, a tool to get stones out of horses' hooves and several knives. It seems strange nowadays that not only was it acceptable back then for Alan to take a knife on a plane and bring it home with-out any trouble, but it was also alright for me to take it to school and show everyone. Things have certainly changed. I think I had several penknives in the juniors; they were never used for anything bad, but they were never used for anything useful either.

Alan joined the ATC (Air Training Corps) for which there was a parade ground nearby. He even had a uniform. Once they had been there for a while, they were allowed to go up in a Chipmunk aircraft and also in gliders. It all appeared too regimented for me, and standing around on a parade ground being shouted at seemed like no fun what-soever, so I never joined.

For a while, in about 1970, I was in the school football team. I can never remember joining, the PE teacher had probably enrolled me, and I can't remember who we played or if we travelled anywhere to other teams' pitches. The one thing that I do remember, though, is that we were playing one day when a plane went over and about thirty Royal Marine parachutists jumped out of it and landed in the field surrounding us. That was very exciting to me back then.

However, it transpired that they'd jumped out in the wrong place. I also recall that one day we had to play football away from an old car that had been set on fire and left on the pitch. In those days old cars seemed to be left where they stood for weeks, months or even years. There was a car dumped in the woods that was there for many years and we all played in it. The headmaster would warn us in assembly not to go anywhere near the car and certain kids who had been spotted near it would be told off.

All kids collected stamps back then. I had a great collection as we had lived in Singapore and Malaya for three years in the 1960s. Dad travelled the world with the Navy so was always sending us back lovely stamps. There were also stamp clubs in all of our comics and they would be given away

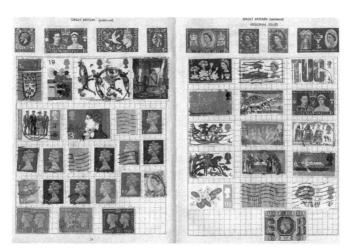

A couple of pages from an old stamp album. Dad would send us many stamps from abroad, as would his friends. The ones shown are all from England, though.

free with cereal. Sometime in the 1970s I must have given all of my stamps away. I can't really remember what happened to them, but I wish I had them now.

We all collected coins, and every kid would have a collection that came from all over the world. Food companies would give away collections of world coins, and I remember that there was confectionary offering banknotes of the world. I had one note from China for about ten years.

Kids collected just about anything in the 1970s, including bubblegum cards, marbles, stickers, badges (I had hundreds), football pendants, cereal toys, Brooke Bond cards, sweet cigarette cards, football coins, soldiers, Cowboys and Indians, etc. Some kids at my junior school collected Robertson's Golly badges and statuettes. One of their aunties had sent Golly statuettes for the whole football team, and he brought them to school to show us. To get a badge or statuette, you had to save endless tokens from Robertson's jam jars. I don't know how his auntie managed to eat so much jam in order to collect for an entire football team!

In the evening, we would sometimes meet up in the junior school playground. I would take Shep up there and we would have a run around. Sometimes we would meet up with other kids and just explore the estate or look for conkers. We never got up to any trouble, apart from knocking on front doors and running off!

We always seemed to be out and about doing something, but at the same time we returned indoors in time for our favourite TV programmes.

Seven

MUSIC

The music of the 1970s was amazing. Not only was it all completely original, but it also started off new trends and fashions. 1970 kicked off with *Love Grows (Where My Rosemary Goes)* by Edison Lighthouse, and the music of the year included a mixture of songs by artists such as Simon & Garfunkel, Dana, the England World Cup Squad, Mungo Jerry and Elvis Presley. Smokey Robinson and The Miracles had a hit called *Tears of a Clown*, and *Paint Your Wagon* with Clint Eastwood had just come out at the cinema. In the film Lee Marvin sang *Wand'rin' Star*, the record proved very popular and it was one of the first singles that I ever bought. Mum and dad had a Dansette record player, but I always had it in my room. I'll always remember putting on Lee Marvin and speeding it up to 78rpm. His voice sounded so comical at that speed that neither Alan nor I could stop laughing, and every time we looked at each other we'd start laughing again. I ended up with hiccups in the end!

We had very few singles in the house. Mum and dad had one by Jim Reeves called *But You Love Me, Daddy*, which we managed to wreck when it got jammed on the player. Our neighbours gave the bulk of their single collection to us. I only remember one of the singles, and that was *A Little Bit Me, A Little Bit You* by The Monkees, which I played over and over. I got to like The Monkees to such an extent that I used to spend all my pocket money buying their old LPs from the second-hand market in town.

One of the first singles that I remember buying on my own was *Leader of the Pack* by The Shangri-Las in 1972, but I must have bought other records before that. Many shops would have booths in them with headphones so that you could listen to new records before buying them. I remember the Boots shop in town had a whole floor that was dedicated to selling records, and every Saturday we would go there and listen to the latest releases. I think in those days a single was about 50 pence and LPs were £2.99, although you could get the cheaper 'Music for Pleasure' albums for £1.99. The MFP albums were always advertised with well-known names on the cover, but when you got them home they were sung by someone else. We used to love getting a new album and looking at the cover; it somehow seemed a lot better than the later, tiny CDs. There must be lots of people around today who miss those old scratchy vinyl records. I certainly do.

As the seventies moved on, Alan started getting music papers like NME, Disco 45 and Sounds. They often had

The 1970s was also when flexi-discs really became popular. These were very thin plastic singles that were often given away with pop magazines or newspapers. Smith's Crisps gave away a selection of them for a while, featuring acts like Slade, the Bay City Rollers, Gary Glitter and Status Quo. The single shown is a flexi-disc, which was given away free with the long-since-disappeared pop magazine, *Popswop*.

This photo shows Noddy Holder appearing on stage with Slade in the early 1970s. Noddy shouting 'It's Christmas!' seems to have kicked off every Christmas ever since, and must have brought in a fortune since it was first recorded.

pullout posters which would go straight onto our bedroom walls. Alan eventually moved out of our room and had his own room, which was covered in Pace posters of Marc Bolan. Pace posters were the best you could get at the time. I think I had *Alias Smith and Jones* posters on my walls.

By then, Alan had the latest stereo record player, which included a built-in radio; this was very modern back then. Now that I had my own room and the Dansette to myself, I must have driven Alan nuts by continually playing The Monkees over and over. But he would retaliate with T. Rex and Slade. It truly was a battle of the bands.

Glam rock really kicked off in about 1972 with artists such as Marc Bolan, Gary Glitter, Alvin Stardust, David

Bowie, Mud, Slade, Roxy Music and Sweet, together with many other bands and artists. With it came crazy fashions, which caught on with everyone, including platform shoes, huge flared trousers and wing-collared shirts. The bigger your platforms, the cooler you were. My platforms had about three-inch heels, which I wore to school until the heels wore out and became completely hollow. I remember telling someone at the bus stop about *Top of the Pops* the night before. Someone said, 'Oh, and there was an old man on there.' The 'old man' turned out to be Alvin Stardust and he became one of my favourite artists. Down came the posters of The Monkees and *Alias Smith and Jones* and up went posters of Alvin Stardust. When his first album came out, mum got me all the promotional stuff that they were throwing out at the shop and I stuck it on my walls. When no one was looking, I would put his record on my Dansette and pretend I was Alvin. I loved it when he came on *Top of the Pops*, as well as many of the other bands.

David Cassidy, Donny Osmond and the Bay City Rollers were huge stars in the early 1970s, and huge crowds of screaming girls gathered wherever they went. When the Bay City Rollers came to Plymouth in 1975, all the girls were talking about it on the school bus. Many had tickets and there were lots of stories about the concert the day after. The Rollers had their own show called *Shang-A-Lang* which ran for twenty weeks and always seemed to be on when I got back from school. The music was certainly varied, and other diverse acts around at the time included The Wombles, Benny Hill, The Goodies, Clive Dunn, Lieutenant Pigeon and Telly Savalas. Every number one reminds me of an event from the 1970s. I knew all the words to Benny Hill's record

Ernie, which went to number one just before Christmas 1971. I remember my mum having the radio on and the DJ introducing it, and I rushed to turn on my dad's reel-to-reel tape recorder. Slade's *Mama Weer All Crazee Now* reminds me of the time mum took me on holiday to Blackpool. The journey was endless and there were no toilets. When we did finally stop at a service station, some of the kids, in crazy 'Oxford Bags' and wild 1970s clothes, rushed to the jukebox and put on Slade. Donny Osmond's *Puppy Love* reminds me of the craze that swept Britain in 1972, which started with Donny Osmond and by the end of the year included his brother, 'Little Jimmy Osmond', who had a hit with *Long Haired Lover From Liverpool* in December.

The first number one of 1970 was *Love Grows (Where My Rosemary Grows)* from Edison Lighthouse, which was followed by Lee Marvin with *Wand'rin' Star*, Simon and Garfunkel with *Bridge Over Troubled Water*, Dana with *All Kinds of Everything*, Norman Greenbaum with *Spirit in the Sky*, the England World Cup Squad 1970 with *Back Home*, Christie with *Yellow River*, Mungo Jerry with *In the Summertime*, Elvis Presley with *The Wonder of You*, Smokey Robinson and The Miracles with *Tears of a Clown*, Freda Payne with *Band of Gold*, Matthews Southern Comfort with *Woodstock* and The Jimi Hendrix Experience with *Voodoo Child*. The Christmas number one of 1970 was *I Hear You Knocking* by Dave Edmunds' Rockpile.

The number ones of 1971 were Clive Dunn with *Grandad* (Dad's Army was still very popular and Dunn played Corporal Jones), George Harrison with *My Sweet Lord*, Mungo Jerry with *Baby Jump*, T. Rex with *Hot Love*, Dave and Ansel Collins with *Double Barrel*, Dawn with *Knock*

Three Times, Middle of the Road with *Chirpy Chirpy Cheep Cheep*, T. Rex again with *Get it On*, Diana Ross with *I'm Still Waiting*, The Tams with *Hey Girl Don't Bother Me*, Rod Stewart with *Maggie May* and Slade with *Coz I Luv You*. My favourite song that year was also the Christmas number one and featured Benny Hill singing *Ernie (The Fastest Milkman in the West)*.

1972's number ones included The New Seekers with *I'd Like to Teach the World to Sing* (which was made popular by the Coke advert), T. Rex with *Telegram Sam* and *Metal Guru* (my brother played them over and over), Chicory Tip with *Son of my Father* (I've still got a free flexi-disc from *Popswop*), Nilsson with *Without You*, The Royal Scots Dragoon Guards with *Amazing Grace*, Don McLean with *Vincent*, Slade with *Take Me Bak 'Ome*, Donny Osmond with *Puppy Love*, Alice Cooper with *School's Out* (which came out in the summer holidays), Rod Stewart with *You Wear it Well*, Slade again with *Mama Weer All Crazee Now*, David Cassidy with *How Can I Be Sure* (all the girls were mad about him at school), Lieutenant Pigeon with *Mouldy Old Dough*, Gilbert O'Sullivan with *Clair* and Chuck Berry with *My Ding-a-Ling* (which Mary Whitehouse tried unsuccessfully to get banned). Little Jimmy Osmond had the end of the year Christmas hit with *Long Haired Lover From Liverpool*.

1973 produced more great bands and songs from artists including Sweet with *Blockbuster*, Slade with *Cum On Feel the Noize*, Donny Osmond with *The Twelfth of Never*, Dawn featuring Tony Orlando with *Tie a Yellow Ribbon Round the Ole Oak Tree*, Wizzard with *See My Baby Jive*, Suzi Quatro with *Can the Can*, 10cc with *Rubber Bullets*, Slade again with *Skweeze Me Pleeze Me*, Peters and Lee with *Welcome Home*,

Gary Glitter with *I'm the Leader of the Gang (I Am!)*, Donny Osmond again with *Young Love*, Wizzard once more with *Angel Fingers*, the Simon Park Orchestra with *Eye Level* (the theme from the popular detective series *Van Der Valk*), David Cassidy with *Daydreamer / The Puppy Song* and Gary Glitter again with *I Love You Love Me Love*.

Just before Christmas, Slade released *Merry Christmas Everybody*, a song that has been played millions of times ever since and continues to be enjoyed.

1974 saw several acts reaching number one for the first time, including Alvin Stardust with *Jealous Mind*, Terry Jacks with *Seasons in the Sun*, Paper Lace with *Billy Don't Be a Hero*, the Rubettes with *Sugar Baby Love*, Ray Stevens with *The Streak*, John Denver with *Annie's Song*, David Essex with *Gonna Make You a Star*, The Three Degrees with *When Will I See You Again*, Ken Boothe with *Everything I Own*, George McCrae with *Rock Your Baby*, Charles Aznavour with *She*, Sweet Sensation with *Sad Sweet Dreamer*, Barry White with *You're the First, the Last, My Everything* and, of course, Abba with *Waterloo*. Regulars in the charts included The New Seekers with *You Won't Find Another Fool Like Me*, Mud with *Tiger Feet*, The Osmonds with *Love Me for a Reason*, Suzi Quatro with *Devil Gate Drive* and Gary Glitter with *Always Yours*. My favourite number one of the year was *Kung Fu Fighting* by Karl Douglas. Everyone loved Kung Fu back then. The TV series with David Carradine was very popular. Mud finished off the year with another ker-ching record, *Lonely This Christmas*.

In 1975 the chart seemed to change a bit. A lot of the glam acts were no longer getting to number one. Number ones that year included Status Quo with *Down Down*, The

Tymes with *Ms Grace*, Pilot with *January*, Steve Harley and Cockney Rebel with *Make Me Smile*, Telly Savalas with *If* (Kojak was huge at the time), the Bay City Rollers with *Bye Bye Baby* and *Give a Little Love*, Mud with *Oh Boy*, Tammy Wynette with *Stand by your Man*, Windsor Davies and Don Estelle with *Whispering Grass* (*It Ain't Half Hot, Mum* was also very popular at the time), 10cc with *I'm Not in Love*, Johnny Nash with *Tears on my Pillow*, Typically Tropical with *Barbados*, The Stylistics with *Can't Give You Anything But My Love*, Rod Stewart with *Sailing*, David Essex with *Hold Me Close*, Art Garfunkel with *I Only Have Eyes For You*, David Bowie with *Space Oddity*, Billy Connolly with *D.I.V.O.R.C.E.* (a parody of Tammy Wynette's hit), and Queen with *Bohemian Rhapsody*.

In 1976 the number ones were Abba with *Mamma Mia*, *Fernando* and *Dancing Queen*, Slik with *Forever and Ever*, The Four Seasons with *December 1963 (Oh What a Night)*, Tina Charles with *I Love to Love (But My Baby Loves to Dance*, Brotherhood of Man with *Save Your Kisses for Me* (the Eurovision Song Contest winner that year), J.J. Barrie with *No Charge*, The Wurzels with *Combine Harvester* (a parody of Melanie's *Brand New Key* hit of the early 1970s), Real Thing with *You to Me are Everything*, Demis Roussos with *The Roussos Phenomenon EP*, Elton John and Kiki Dee with *Don't Go Breaking My Heart*, Pussycat with *Mississippi*, Chicago with *If You Leave Me Now*, Showaddywaddy with *Under the Moon of Love*, and the Christmas hit was from Johnny Mathis with *When a Child is Born*.

In 1977 the first number one was David Soul with *Don't Give Up On Us* (*Starsky and Hutch* was the most watched show at the time), followed by Julie Covington with

Don't Cry for Me, Argentina, Leo Sayer with *When I Need You*, Manhattan Transfer with *Chanson D'Amour*, Deniece Williams with *Free*, Rod Stewart with *I Don't Want to Talk About It / The First Cut is the Deepest*, Kenny Rogers with *Lucille*, The Jacksons with *Show You the Way to Go*, Hot Chocolate with *So You Win Again*, Donna Summer with *I Feel Love*, Brotherhood of Man with *Angelo* (the group were turning into the British Abba for a while), The Floaters with *Float On*, Elvis Presley with *Way Down* (Elvis had just died), David Soul again with *Silver Lady*, Baccara with *Yes Sir, I Can Boogie* and Abba with *The Name of the Game*. The Christmas number one was Wings with *Mull of Kintyre / Girls School*.

The first number one of 1978 was Anthea and Donna with *Uptown Top Ranking*, followed by Brotherhood of Man with *Figaro*, Abba with *Take a Chance on Me*, Kate Bush with *Wuthering Heights*, Brian and Michael with *Matchstalk Men and Matchstalk Cats and Dogs* (a song about the painter, Lowry), the Bee Gees with *Night Fever* (*Saturday Night Fever* with John Travolta was the year's big hit), Boney M with *Rivers of Babylon*, John Travolta and Olivia Newton-John with *You're the One that I Want* (from Travolta's other big movie hit of the year, *Grease*), the Commodores with *Three Times a Lady*, 10cc with *Dreadlock Holiday*, John Travolta and Olivia Newton-John again, this time with *Summer Nights* (another hit from *Grease*), The Boomtown Rats with *Rat Trap*, Rod Stewart with *Do Ya Think I'm Sexy* and the Christmas hit was Boney M again with *Mary's Boy Child – Oh My Lord*.

1979's first number one was from the Village People with *YMCA*, followed by Ian Dury and the Blockheads with *Hit*

Hugh Cornwell on stage performing with The Stranglers in 1977. The Stranglers had many hits including 'No More Heroes', 'Peaches', 'Strange Little Girl' and 'Duchess'.

Me with your Rhythm Stick, Blondie with *Heart of Glass*, the Bee Gees with *Tragedy*, Gloria Gaynor with *I Will Survive*, Art Garfunkel with *Bright Eyes*, Blondie again with *Sunday Girl*, Anita Ward with *Ring My Bell*, Tubeway Army with *Are Friends Electric*, The Boomtown Rats with *I Don't Like Mondays*, Cliff Richard with *We Don't Talk Anymore*, Gary Numan with *Cars*, The Police with *Message in a Bottle*, The Buggles with *Video Killed the Radio Star*, Lena Martell with *One Day at a Time*, Dr Hook with *When You're in Love with a Beautiful Woman* and The Police again with *Walking on the Moon*. The very last number one of 1979 and the 1970s was Pink Floyd with *Another Brick in the Wall*.

Few bands made it through the seventies, but two that did were Queen and Abba. Abba had won the Eurovision

Song Contest with *Waterloo* in 1974. Back then, everybody watched the Eurovision Song Contest – it was a TV highlight every year. The other memorable 1970s artists who won were Dana with *All Kinds of Everything*, which was a hit in 1970, and Brotherhood of Man with *Save Your Kisses for Me* in 1976.

Glam rock slowly died off and was followed by punk rock and disco music. The main punk bands included The Sex Pistols, The Damned, The Stranglers, The Clash, and popular artists at the time included Elvis Costello and Ian Dury. The Americans jumped on the bandwagon with groups like Blondie and the Ramones.

The year 1977 was an odd one for music. Elvis Presley died in August, and many people were into rock 'n' roll, but in the same year there was also punk music, so the charts went from one extreme to the other. There was also Abba, whose music was totally different again. Later in the year, Marc Bolan died in a car crash, and the following month Bing Crosby died on a golf course. Bing Crosby isn't a name that you associate with the 1970s straight away, but he had a huge hit with David Bowie in 1977 just before he died.

I remember that during 1977 there were many punks, complete with colourful Mohican haircuts, who would all meet up outside the Virgin store in town. I think that many people were reluctant to pass them, but on the whole they were completely harmless. There used to be a teenager who lived near us who would walk up to the newsagent to get the paper dressed in a German SS uniform. All the older people had known him as a kid and just said 'hello' to him as if he was dressed normally. It seemed odd that people who had been through the war would be happy with an

SS officer in front of them in the queue. At the same time there were a few teddy boys with Brylcreemed hair. Rock 'n' roll had made a comeback in the 1970s with acts like Bill Haley, Buddy Holly and, of course, Elvis Presley being in the charts. Rock 'n' roll bands included Showaddywaddy, The Darts and Mud. Shows like *Happy Days* also added to the appeal.

The end of the 1970s produced some great bands like The Police, Madness, The Jam, The Specials and The Undertones. The music at the end of the 1970s was totally different to the music at the beginning of the decade, and my favourite period will always be the glam rock era. It's hard today to imagine that it will ever be repeated.

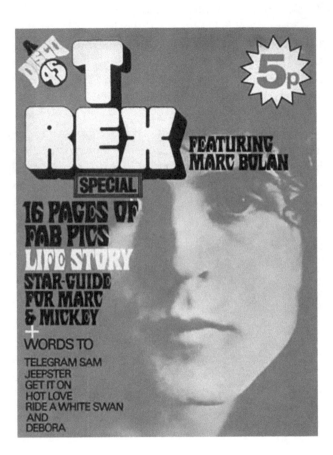

DISCO 45

5p

T REX SPECIAL

FEATURING MARC BOLAN

16 PAGES OF FAB PICS
LIFE STORY
STAR-GUIDE FOR MARC & MICKEY
+
WORDS TO

TELEGRAM SAM
JEEPSTER
GET IT ON
HOT LOVE
RIDE A WHITE SWAN
AND
DEBORA

Eight

FASHIONS

Everyone remembers the fashions of the 1970s, especially the platform shoes and flared trousers. The beginning of the 1970s started with fashions left over from the 1960s; the mini-skirt was just going out (although still remained) and the midi and maxi were coming in. Hot pants became popular for girls and bell-bottoms or flares became more popular with men.

Everyone had platforms. Kids everywhere would clonk around like Frankenstein. I remember getting my first pair of platforms at school and I wore them everywhere. Eventually, the heels wore out, and by then the fashion seemed to be over. At the bus stop, we'd all compare our shoes, which were varying colours of leather, mainly reddish brown and greenish brown.

A pair of girls' platform shoes.

I remember a girl falling off her platform shoes at school and either twisting or breaking her ankle. The deputy head consequently decided that pupils could only wear platforms of a certain size. What with having our platforms, our flares and our hair measured, as well as having our socks checked to make sure they weren't white, it all got a bit ridiculous. Kids would wear their biggest platforms to school just to annoy the teachers. For a while, we were all about 6ft 3!

We all lost a few inches in height when the fashion for platforms died out. Even our school shirts followed fashion and every week the collars would steadily get bigger and bigger. The fashions not only affected the kids and teen-agers but adults as well. It was impossible to get a pair of trousers that weren't flared in the middle of the 1970s. Boys used to measure their flares to see who had the biggest and also boasted about who had the most buttons on their high-waisted trousers. Checked trousers and tartan ones (especially when the Bay City Rollers were big) were also

I actually had a pair of trousers identical to the ones shown in this advert from about 1975. I wonder what happened to them? I thought they were great at the time.

very popular, as were Oxford Bags with huge baggy, flared legs, often in a checked pattern with very deep pockets.

We all grew our hair in about 1973, much to the annoyance of the teachers who would, as mentioned earlier, measure it regularly with a ruler to check that it wasn't too long. Some kids were even ordered home to get their hair cut.

Shirts featured loud patterns at the time. I remember Alan had a shirt with drawings of Laurel and Hardy all over it. Tank tops were also in and worn by everyone in the early 1970s, and cheesecloth and denim were very popular, too.

Even underpants appeared in wacky psychedelic colours with weird patterns, including purple or mustard. Other pants had Beethoven on them or the Union Jack.

Skinheads wore tight denim jeans and bovver boots (Doc Martens), together with buttoned-up shirts and sometimes braces.

Kipper ties were in for a while, but then for a short time ties seemed to disappear altogether. Many shops, discos and clubs seemed to be inhabited by men with unbuttoned shirts, hairy chests and crucifixes around their necks. Kids copied this (minus the hairy chests), and many also wore medallions around their necks to school.

Punk brought its own fashion, with people having Mohican haircuts, ripped t-shirts, tartan bondage trousers and safety pins through their noses. For the first and last time bin liners became fashionable. It was definitely a fashion taken up by only a select few and was never as popular as the other crazy fashions earlier on in the 1970s. Occasionally, there would be a group of punks in the town, but there were never really that many. It was a lot more popular in London.

A busy summer's day on Plymouth Hoe. Smeaton's Tower can be seen in the background. Many people are sunbathing, some in deckchairs, and many of the older men are wearing suits.

This photo shows students mimicking the mannequins in the shop window behind them. Plenty of 1970s fashion on show here, including huge flares. The mannequins have wild 'Jason King' type hair, and are wearing shirts with wing-collars, kipper ties and typical 1970s suits. There are also some Oxford Bags hanging up, which appear to be £5.25. The suit is £18.50, a shirt is £2.75 and a kipper tie is £1.50 (a bargain). All this and Green Shield Stamps as well!

Later in the 1970s, drainpipes were back and the fifties seemed to be in fashion again. If you had worn some of the fashions from the early 1970s in the late 1970s, you would have been ridiculed. Films like *Saturday Night Fever* with John Travolta portrayed disco fashion and this soon took off.

Short-sleeved t-shirts with iron-on transfers were very popular in the late 1970s. Tight-fitting t-shirts with numbers on (similar to baseball shirts) or transfers of popular TV programmes like *Starsky and Hutch*, *The Six Million Dollar Man* or *Charlie's Angels* were worn everywhere. Other t-shirts had slogans (some rude), such as, 'I'm with this idiot' (together with a hand pointing right), 'Keep death off the road – Drive on the pavement!' and 'Reality is an illusion caused by the lack of alcohol'. Other popular t-shirt designs featured pop stars, popular films, cars, drink, Superman, Union Jacks and even the Queen's Silver Jubilee.

Groups like The Jam, Madness and The Specials led to a mod revival, but the fifties theme continued, especially after Elvis died.

The Very Big Brontosaurus

There once was a Brontosaurus who was enormously big. And people all around led expeditions up his north face (which was the most difficult way). They'd start at the tip of his tail, onto his back, then there was the almost vertical climb up his neck, (a lot of people gave up there) finally finishing up on top of his head.

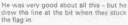

He was very good about all this – but he drew the line at the bit when they stuck the flag in.

Then he'd tilt his head back with a smirk and they'd all slide down his long neck and land with a bump on his back. Perhaps one day someone will manage to stick the flag on his head. When he's having a snooze.

Cadbury Limited, Bournville, Birmingham

Please dispose of this wrapper carefully 'Keep Britain Tidy'

Nine

SWEETS AND CHOCOLATE

There were many different sweets and chocolates during the 1970s. I loved them all! Curly Wurlys were launched in 1970 and the TV advert featured Terry Scott as an over-sized schoolboy with the catchphrase, 'Hands off my Curly Wurly'. The advert for Cadbury's Fruit & Nut featured Frank Muir and there were badges and other promotional items issued at the time.

There were also Picnic, Ice Breaker, Fry's Chocolate Cream, Crunchie, Turkish Delight, Maltesers, Rolos, Marathon (which later became Snickers), Revels, Treets and Wagon Wheels.

Mum used to give me a Wagon Wheel to take to school every day. It's true what they say – they were certainly a lot bigger back then. You used to get strawberry ones, too;

Some of the badges we collected as kids featured our favourite sweets and chocolates, as well as other memorable items from the 1970s, including badges for Hot Wheels, Clarks Commandos, fireworks, crisps and Smash.

perhaps you still do, but it's a long time since I last had one. They were all wrapped in wax paper back then. There certainly weren't as many plastic wrappers as there are today. All chocolate bars were sold in ones, you couldn't get them in huge packs like you do now. All chocolate bars came in their own paper wrappers like Penguins, Mars Bars and Marathon, and some also came in silver paper like Kit Kat, Dairy Milk and Galaxy.

Popular chocolate bars included Waifa, Nutty, Twix, Caramel, Bar Six, Aero, Dairy Crunch, Yorkie, Topic, Swisskit, Buttersnap, Caramac, Milky Bar, Welcome, Rumba, Toffee Crisp, Prize, Bounty, Flake, Dipped Flake, Drifter, Texan, Fruit and Nut and many others.

There used to be many toffee bars and nougat bars that mum would give me to take to school. I remember Arrow Bars, which were a halfpenny before decimalisation and became Penny Arrows afterwards. They came in many flavours including nutty toffee and fruit salad.

For our mums and dads, there were After Eights, Milk Tray, Old Jamaica, Dairy Box, Black Magic, Grande Seville and Matchmakers (which came in various flavours including mint, orange and coffee).

Sweets included Opal Fruits, Spangles, Refreshers, Lovehearts, Fruit Pastilles, Pacers, Fruit Gums, Tooty Frooties, Laughs, Jelly Babies and Wine Gums.

TV programmes would sometimes influence what sweets we bought. For a while, when *Kojak* was on, many kids would walk around sucking lollipops because they thought that it made them look cool.

We'd all buy sweet cigarettes and pretend to be characters from the TV programmes and movies that were on at the time. Sweet cigarettes also included trading cards from popular TV shows and films, such as *James Bond*, *Dad's Army* and *Space 1999*.

Popular sweets bought from the shop near to our comprehensive school included Blackjacks and Fruit Salads (you could get eight for a penny), flying saucers, milk bottles, chocolate mice, lemon bon bons, liquorice boot laces and pear drops.

We all ate Bazooka Joe bubblegum, and the wrappers – that were also little comics – could be found in the streets everywhere. If you saved the wrappers, you could send away for free gifts. I think that I sent away for a pair of binoculars, which were never any good and fell apart soon after I got them. Collecting bubblegum cards was a popular pastime. I can still remember the taste of the gum that you got with them. Of course, we weren't interested in the

A selection of my favourite bars of chocolate from the 1970s. Curly Wurly and Milky Way are still for sale today, but the others have long since disappeared. After Jon Pertwee left Doctor Who, there was also a chocolate bar featuring Tom Baker as the Doctor.

gum, just the cards, which would be swapped with all our friends so that we could try and get the complete set. Cards either featured a popular TV series or were of footballers. There must have been endless sets of footballer cards. The bubblegum cards that I can remember collecting in the 1970s were of *Kojak*, *The Six Million Dollar Man*, *Kung Fu* and *Planet of the Apes*.

Pirate Bags or Lucky Bags were also very popular. At the beginning of the 1970s, they cost 1s (or 5 pence) and contained sweets and a toy.

Other long-forgotten chocolate bars include Pink Panther bars (bright pink chocolate), Cabanas (coconut, cherry, caramel and chocolate), Aztec, Amazin' Raisin, Fry's 5 Boys, the Milk Tray block, The Wombles, Peanut Extra, Golden Crisp (5 pence), Bourneville Dark, Club Orange, Golden Cup (3 pence), Galaxy Counters (with a strange bird on the packet), Fudge, Drifter, Nestlé Doctor Who milk chocolate (with a drawing of Jon Pertwee on the front), Fry's chocolate cream and Fry's peppermint cream (both 3½ pence), Lion bar, Milky Way (2 pence), Cadbury's Oranges and Lemons (5 pence), Terry's Bitz, Fry's Tiffin and Toffee Buttons.

Unsurprisingly, like most kids in the 1970s, I tried them all.

Ten

HOUSEHOLD SHOPPING

In the early 1970s, there were no superstores anywhere. Our nearby shops included a newsagent, a Liptons, two butchers, a Make and Mend shop, a wool shop, a Mace and a toyshop. All areas had a selection of shops like this and most food was bought locally. There were no shops selling frozen food in bulk, and the most you could get were Birdseye fish fingers or something similar. Because of this, everyone just had a small fridge with a tiny freezer department at the top. Large freezers were unheard of.

On Saturday, we would all go off into town, either by car or bus, and have a meal at the Magnet Restaurant. Most families did the same. Our jaunts into town weren't to stock up on food, but were to get other bits and pieces needed around the house and also to buy new clothes.

The more instant something was, the more appeal it seemed to have, so items such as instant coffee, instant potato, instant whip and Angel Delight all took off.

Pizzas became popular in the 1970s and we all loved them. It seemed like a little piece of America (even though they were Italian). I remember the first pizza we ever had, and the reason was because a kid at school wanted to do cookery evening classes and roped me in. In those days, no boys took cooking (or domestic science as it was known). It's amazing that I ever went because I hated school and have never been particularly interested in cooking. We made a few things, including a sponge roll (mine was like cardboard), pancakes (I dropped mine on the floor) and, of course, the pizza, which I took home and we all ate. Mum bought her pizzas in town from then on, but they were different from the ones you get today. One I remember from Marks and Spencer had mince on – a strange combination.

Other 1970s foods that I can recall included Cadbury's Smash (which took off when the advert with the robots appeared on TV) and Fray Bentos pies (I loved them), chicken kievs, lasagne, moussaka, prawn cocktails, quiche lorraine, salmon mousse (yuk!), sardine eggs, scampi, chicken supreme, pate and ratatouille. I can also remember when Vesta curries came out and they seemed very popular for a while.

Fondue sets took off at one time, used for meat, cheese or chocolate (although not at the same time).

Popular cereals included Puffa Puffa Rice, Ricicles, Corn Flakes, Golden Nuggets (much better than they are now), Country Store, Alpen, Puffed Wheat, Quaker Oats, Weetabix, Oat Krunchies, Shreddies, Special K (totally different from today's cereal of the same name), Quaker Natural Cereal, Prewett's Wholewheat Flakes, Variety Packs (which were called 'Sweet Six'), Grape Nuts, Eight to One (the best muesli ever), Sugar Puffs, Sugar Smacks, Coco Krispies and Kellogg's Sugar Stars (with Sooty on the front). It might be an age thing, but all these brands seemed to taste a lot better to me back in the 1970s.

Biscuits included Nabisco's Magic Roundabout Malted Milk, Cadbury's Cookies and McVitie's Digestives, as well as many other brands that are still around today.

Drinks included Robinson's Lemon Barley Water, Tree Top Orange Drink, Ribena, Kellogg's Rise and Shine and Just Juice, together with fizzy drinks like Coke, Cresta and 7-Up.

We all loved crisps, and the main brands were Smith's and Golden Wonder. Available at the time were Smith's Horror Bags, which came in several varieties, including Bones, Claws, Bats, Fangs and Ribs. For a while they even came with a free horror mask.

There were also bacon-flavoured Frazzles, All Stars (again bacon flavour), Atom Smashers (with free space stickers), Monster Munch, Quavers, Wotsits, Wigwams and Hula Hoops. Golden Wonder produced the usual flavours of the time, such as Beef and Onion, Ready Salted, Cheese and Onion, and Salt and Vinegar. Smith's produced similar flavours, as well as Chipsticks (Maize and Potato). I liked Smith's crisps because there always seemed to be a competition or free pop records when you collected the tokens from the packs. I remember kids would roam the streets searching for discarded crisp packets so that they could cut off the coupons and send off for a free flexi-disc featuring the latest bands.

Kids were crazy about badges, and many products came with their own badges which would be given away free with the product, especially in shops which sold Wall's and Lyons Maid. I loved them all. With mum working in a shop that sold ice cream, I always managed to get the full set!

Ice cream could be bought in blocks from the local grocery shop and included vanilla, Wall's raspberry ripple and neapolitan.

Also, for dessert you could have Angel Delight, Instant Whip, Arctic roll, brandy snaps, apple strudel, baked Alaska, caramel oranges, lemon soufflé and profiteroles.

Snacks included Peek Freans' Twiglets, Energen cheese crispbread, Energen rye crispbread and various cheese biscuits like Cheddars and Tuc.

Breville introduced the sandwich toaster in the early 1970s and every family had to have one. Most families used it once or twice, got fed up with cleaning it, and then shoved it to the back of the cupboard and forgot about it – like a lot of 1970s novelty gadgets!

Washing powders included Omo, Daz, Drive, Radiant, Aerial and 'Square Deal' Surf.

Huge cans of beer included Watney's 'Party Four' and 'Jumbo 4 – Real Draught Bitter'.

Towards the end of the 1970s, 'freezer centres' opened selling all sorts of frozen food. Mum and dad bought a full-size freezer, as many families did back then, which wasn't upright and you had to lean into it to get the food out. I remember we had it when mum won her trolley dash competition in the local Co-op. She had to collect as much food as she could in fifteen minutes, but it had to add up to no more than £100, which seemed a fortune in those days. The freezer seemed to be full for months afterwards.

At Christmas, the meal was much the same as it is today, with turkey, potatoes, Brussels sprouts and gravy which would be made with either Bisto or Oxo. Party food included vol-au-vents, Scotch eggs, pork pies, meatballs, mini sausage rolls and cheese and olives (or pineapple) on a stick.

I suppose the 1970s was also the time when fast food was first introduced to Britain. The Magnet Restaurant that we went to every Saturday closed and a Wimpy Bar opened up in town. On occasion, Dad would take me down there and I would always order a cheeseburger, which at the time cost 26 pence. Although they called themselves fast food restau-

A 1970s Childhood

rants, you had to wait at least forty minutes before you got your burger. It's funny; I've never tasted burgers like them since.

For a while, towards the end of the 1970s, Alan got a job running a burger van. He used to come home stinking of it. Some evenings we would go into town and buy a burger off him. It wasn't the safest of jobs and sometimes he would come under attack and the burger van would be turned on its side by yobs. I can't remember how long he did that job for, but I do remember the smell!

Of course, a lot of the foods that were available in the 1970s are still available today, but I'm pretty sure that they taste nothing like they did back then.

We loved visits from the ice-cream man, who seemed to drive along our street every day in the summer holidays. Many ice creams and lollies have changed over the years, but back then the ice-cream vans all served Wall's, Lyons Maid or Mr Whippy.

Popular lollies at the time were Funny Feet, Haunted House, Zoom, Orange Dragon, Captain Cody, Jelly Terror, Orange Quench (which cost 10d in 1970), Jungle Bar (which contained strawberry and cost 7d), Super Orange Maid (which cost 1s), Frutie Blue (which was 2 pence in 1971), Cola Rola (also 2 pence), Squeezes (which included lemon, lime and grapefruit and cost 5 pence), Chocolate Glory and Strawberry Glory (both 7 pence), Mr Merlin's Magic Purple Potion (3 pence), Super Zoom, Black Prince, Jungle Jim, Totem Pole, Choco, Angel, Jack of Diamonds, Nut Cracker, Freckles, Freak Out, Blackcurrant and Cola Smash, Captain Rainbow, Crime Squad and many more. I don't remember all of them, but I'm pretty sure that we would have tried each one at some time or another. Due to the popularity of *Doctor Who*, Wall's brought out Dalek's Death Ray, which included chocolate and mint.

Popular ice-cream cones included Cornish Ice Cream, Mr Whippy and 99s, which of course came with a flake.

You could also get various blocks of ice cream to store in your tiny freezer compartment. Back then, they were called 'slabs' and 'bricks', and popular ones were Strawberry 'n' Pear (costing 2/6d in 1970), Cassata (vanilla and chocolate with a tutti frutti centre with cherries, sultanas and angelica, costing 3/3d), and Serve and Serve Again (which was a double-sized ice-cream pack which cost 24 pence in 1971). There were many, many more. It seemed special having your own supply of ice cream stored in the freezer rather than having to wait for the daily visit from the ice-cream man.

Another product was frozen mousse, which came in three flavours — lemon, strawberry and chocolate, and each was shaped as a racing car or a boat. Later, there was New Taste Mouse, which came in various flavours, and Sweet Treats, which was another mousse-based product.

Eleven

COMICS

My favourite comic at the beginning of the 1970s was definitely *The Beano*. It used to be delivered every Wednesday and cost 4d. As soon as it came I would read it from cover to cover. My favourite character, of course, was Biffo the Bear and the comic also featured The Bash Street Kids, Little Plum (the son of a Red Indian), Dennis the Menace, Lord Snooty, Billy Whizz, Minnie the Minx (who was just a female Dennis the Menace), Pup Parade (featuring the Bash Street Dogs), Roger the Dodger, Toots (similar to Minnie the Minx) and The Three Bears. All but Biffo the Bear and The Three Bears featured very naughty kids and all seemed to have a lot in common. Some weeks I would get *The Dandy* as well as *The Beano*, which included the adventures of Korky the Cat, Desperate Dan (my favourite),

A collection of my favourite annuals from the 1970s. One day, I'll read them all again!

Dinah Mite, The Smasher (a bully who looked something like Dennis the Menace), Corporal Clott, Bully Beef and Chips, Dirty Dick (who looked just like a kid in my class), Brassneck (a robot schoolboy), Greedy Pigg (a forever hungry teacher), Smarty Gran'pa, Winker Watson and Spunky and his Spider. It all looks very dated nowadays. We used to get all the annuals for Christmas and they would keep me quiet all afternoon.

By 1971, I was reading *Whizzer and Chips*, which featured two comics. Whizzer, with its 'whizz-kids', was run by Sid (from the comic strip 'Sid's Snake') and Chips, with its 'chip-ites', was run by Shiner (who also had his own strip). The comic included Me and My Shadow, Minnie's Mixer, King of the Jungle, Jimmy Jeckle and Master Hide, Slowcoach, Odd-ball, Little Saver, The Champ, Knight School and many more. One strip featured The Spectacular Adventures of Willie Bunk who saw the world through different eyes whenever he put his magic specs on. Also, in 1970, *Cor!!* came out and I bought the first few copies. No 1's free gift was 'Gulp' powder, which when added to water became orange juice. No 2's free gift was a 'Bell boy' bubblegum sweet and No 3 had a free 'Ratty Rasper', which was a piece of card with a rubber band and a metal hoop fixed to it which you wound to make a rasping noise. We all thought that this was fantastic back then. The comic featured Gus the Gorilla, Teacher's Pet, Dogsbodies Academy (a school for dogs), Ivor Lott and Tony Broke, Tricky Dicky, Freddie Fang – The Werewolf Cub (he does a bad deed every day), Jack Pott, Nobby's Hobbies, Donovan's Dad and Whacky (whose dad constantly whacked him and would probably be arrested nowadays). The comic lasted for a few years before becoming amalgamated with *Buster*. I didn't buy it regularly, just when it had free gifts. Those gifts seemed fantastic to us at the time but don't sound too great today. Other favourite comics of that year included *Topper* and *Beezer*.

By 1972 I was reading comics like *TV Comic, Countdown* and *Target*, as well as American comics like *Superman, Batman* and *The Flintstones*. I loved American comics. My friend David's auntie sent him *Casper the Ghost* comics from Canada. For some strange reason, the customs people always removed the cover. For a while I loved *Archie* comics and would be up at the newsagents with my pocket money buying new copies whenever I could. During one summer holiday, mum would buy me a *Superman* comic and make me a hamburger for dinner, which made me feel just like the characters in the comic book!

As the 1970s moved on, I read *Look-in* for a long time. I loved the artwork on the front and all the strips featuring the latest TV characters. Comics were always at their best when they offered a free gift. One issue of *Look-in* featured David Carradine in *Kung Fu* on the front and a free Dragon medallion inside. I think that I bought three copies. I remember wearing the medallion all day around my neck at school.

I'd always loved Marvel comics and in about 1975 Marvel introduced their comics to Britain. I loved the ones featuring Spiderman and the Incredible Hulk. I must have had dozens of copies. Later on, they issued a *Planet of the Apes* comic, which was popular for a while when the show was on the TV. I remember the free gift that came with the first issue of the *Incredible Hulk*; it was an iron-on transfer of the Hulk for your t-shirt. Mum was doing something else so I decided to iron the transfer onto my favourite t-shirt myself. Anyway, the result was that the t-shirt melted! It must have been made of nylon or something similar.

I also bought Marvel's *Fantastic Four* comic and inside you could send away for a mobile featuring your favourite characters. To save time, I decided to trace the characters from the comic and make my own mobile. Unfortunately, I pressed a bit too hard and the indentation of 'The Thing' is still impressed into my parents' teak dining-room table today! I wonder if they ever noticed.

I carried on getting the odd copy of *Look-in* in the later 1970s. It went on well into the 1980s, but by then it had lost a lot of its appeal and I'd long since grown out of reading comics.

countdown
annual

for TV action

UFO·Thunderbirds
The Persuaders·Dr.Who
and other TV favourites

Twelve

TELEVISION

There's no doubt that I loved TV when I was a kid. In those days, we all had black and white sets that were always rented from a local store such as DER, Rumbelows or Granada. All the TVs had a dial tuner and you had to get up and turn it to find the next station. This was usually my job. There were only three channels: BBC1, BBC2 and ITV, which locally for us was Westward Television. Westward had its own evening programme called Westward Diary and things would often go wrong. I remember one show in which everything broke down, so the anchorman, Ken MacLeod, spent the whole programme talking to his co-presenter, Lawrie Quayle, about his holiday in Spain.

The TV programmes in the 1970s were some of the best. I remember running home from school and getting back before my mum, who was working in the shop. Alan would still be at school, so I'd turn the TV on and watch *Paulus the Wood Gnome*, which was a creepy Dutch puppet show. It always seemed to be on. Another show I enjoyed was *Magpie* (mainly for Jenny Hanley), although I was never a *Blue Peter* fan. But my favourite was *Timeslip*, which I never missed. I taped the episodes on my dad's old reel-to-reel tape recorder, and would listen to them all later on. It wasn't an easy process because everyone would have to be quiet when it was recording, and usually Alan would come in and make funny noises.

Another favourite show from 1970 was *UFO*. It was set in the far distant future of 1980 when it was predicted that we would all wear trouser suits, have our hair combed forward, drive snazzy cars and have a base on the moon. *UFO* had all the kids in my class looking skywards for flying saucers, and there were many books about UFOs, one of which was featured on *Magpie*. I also loved *Catweazle*, *Ace of Wands*, *The Tomorrow People*, *Follyfoot* and *Black Beauty* in the early 1970s.

Here is the TV guide that was featured in *Look-in* for a week during 1971:

Saturday

12.50 p.m.	World of Sport
5.15	Shane
6.45	It's Tarbuck

Sunday

1.00 p.m.	Play Better Tennis
2.15	U.N.C.L.E.
3.10	The Big Match

4.05	Cartoon Time
4.40	The Golden Shot
5.35	Catweazle

Monday

3.55 p.m.	Once Upon A Time
4.05	Gus Honeybun
4.45	The Forest Rangers
5.10	Timeslip
6.45	David Nixon's Magic Box

Tuesday

3.55 p.m.	The Enchanted House
4.05	Gus Honeybun
4.50	Junior Showtime
5.10	Magpie
7.00	Star Movie

Wednesday

3.55 p.m.	Rupert Bear
4.05	Gus Honeybun
4.50	The Sooty Show
5.15	Sexton Blake
7.00	Treasure Hunt
8.00	It Takes a Thief

Thursday

3.55 p.m.	Origami
4.05	Gus Honeybun
4.45	Skippy
5.10	Magpie

7.00 p.m.	Film
8.30	This is Your Life

Friday

3.55 p.m.	Zingalong
4.05	Gus Honeybun
4.15	The Ghost and Mrs Muir
4.50	Lost in Space
7.00	The Sky's the Limit

Of course, *Look-in*, being the junior *TV Times*, only featured ITV programmes that they thought would be of interest to children. This selection comes from the Westward TV region, and there were variations up and down the country. Other shows shown elsewhere in the same week included *Voyage to the Bottom of the Sea, Joe 90, The Saint, Robin Hood, Bonanza, Flipper, Stingray, Nanny and the Professor, The Champions, Captain Scarlet, Hogan's Heroes, Man in a Suitcase, Felix the Cat, Department S, UFO, Thunderbirds*, and *Randall and Hopkirk (Deceased)*. Many of these shows had been made in the 1960s, but were still very popular with kids in the 1970s.

Adult comedies in the 1970s included *The Benny Hill Show, Love Thy Neighbour, Bless This House, Man about the House, On the Buses* and *Doctor at Large*. We enjoyed every one!

The Comedians featured comics of the day, including Ken Goodwin ('Settle down now!'), Frank Carson ('It's the way I tell 'em!'), Bernard Manning, Colin Crompton, Stan Boardman, Jim Bowen, George Roper, Duggie Brown, Jimmy Marshall, Tom O'Connor, Mike Reid ('Wallopp!') and Charlie Williams. Comic shows were very popular then and other well-viewed shows included *Dave Allen at Large*, *Freddie Starr* and *The Les Dawson Show*. Les Dawson would tell jokes about his mother-in-law, take part in sketches and appeared as his own superhero, 'Super Flop'. This led to kids in the playground jumping on other kids' backs, shouting the catchphrase, 'SuperFlop!' Like Benny Hill, Les Dawson had his own comic strip in the popular boys' magazine, *Look-in*. The *Look-in* comedy annual of 1974 revealed the most popular acts of the time. Included within its pages were Benny Hill, Charlie Drake, *Doctor at Sea* (with Robin Nedwell, Geoffrey Davies and Ernest Clark), Jimmy Tarbuck, *Bless This House*, *The Comedians*, *Some Mothers Do 'Ave 'Em* (with Michael Crawford), *Please Sir!* (with John Alderton and Deryck Guyler), *Morecambe and Wise*, *Jokers Wild* (which featured Michael Aspel, Les Dawson, Alfred Marks, Clive Dunn, Norman Vaughan, Jack Douglas and Barry Cryer), Les Dawson (whose show 'Sez Les' was very popular at the time), *Man About the House* (with Richard O'Sullivan, Paula Wilcox and Sally Thomsett), Tommy Cooper, Bob Monkhouse (with his cartoon show *Quick on the Draw* which featured Spike Milligan and Leslie Crowther), Freddie Starr, *The Goodies*, Dick Emery, *The Two Ronnies*, *Billy Liar* (which starred Jeff Rawle), *Father Dear Father* (with Patrick Cargill, Ann Holloway and Natasha Pyne), Mike and Bernie Winters and Stanley Baxter.

Who Do You Do? featured impressionists, many long forgotten, such as Dailey and Wayne, Roger Kitter, Janet Brown, Clive Lea, Peter Goodwright and Paul Melba.

Catchphrases were at their best in the 1970s, and nearly all came from TV programmes. Bruce Forsythe's was 'Good game, good game' or 'Nice to see you, to see you nice'. Larry Grayson's were 'What a gay day!' and 'Look at the muck in here', and the very popular *Some Mother's Do 'Ave 'Em* led to the catchphrase 'Ooh, Betty!' All were repeated in the playground the day after the shows were shown. Others included 'Stupid boy!' (from *Dad's Army*), 'Just like that!' (Tommy Cooper), 'It's the way I tell 'em' (Frank Carson), 'I'm free!' (*Are You Being Served?*), 'Shut up!' and 'Lah de dah, Gunner Graham' (from *It Ain't Half Hot, Mum!*) and many more. *Love Thy Neighbour* spawned many catchphrases that couldn't be repeated nowadays, but one that everyone remembers is 'I'll have half', spoken by the character Jacko Robinson in reference to his half-pint of beer.

Everyone loved Sid James from the *Carry On* films, and when he got his own show, *Bless This House*, which also starred Diana Coupland, Robin Stewart and Sally Geeson, it became an instant hit. Sid James played Sidney Abbott and the show revolved around his home life and everything that went with it. I remember an episode where he and his neighbour, Trevor, made an illicit still in the shed and ended up blowing everything to pieces.

Other popular 1970s comedies included *Rising Damp* and *The Rise and Fall of Reginald Perrin*. All featured excellent comedians and it's sad today that most of them are no longer around.

Ronnie Barker was not only excellent in *The Two Ronnies*, but also in *Porridge* where he played 'Fletch'. The show is still shown today and is still as funny as it was back then. Like many of the popular TV programmes of the 1970s, it led to a film being made which was shown at the cinema. *Porridge* also had a spin-off series produced called *Going*

Straight, where Fletch continues life on the outside. It was never as popular as *Porridge* and never gets an airing nowadays. *The Rise and Fall of Reginald Perrin* was also excellent, far better than its imitators, but even that went on a bit too long and lost a lot of its edge in the later series.

In the early 1970s, local TV stations turned to colour. It didn't really matter because everyone still had black and white sets. Turning on *Westward Diary* on the night they changed to colour was hilarious, though. Even though we only had a black and white set, it was obvious that the presenters all had heavy make-up and lipstick on. And that was just the men! Once colour had been around for a few weeks, and people had written in, the make-up was slowly toned down.

Colour TVs cost around £400 then, which at the time was a lot of money. I remember the first family in our street to get one. All the kids were invited to see it. Mum later asked me what I thought of it and I said, 'It's rubbish! Everyone's orange!' What the family who bought it hadn't realised was that you could adjust the colour, and they still had it set as high as it would go.

Mum would take us to the pictures nearly every week, as there was a cinema just down the road. We would see all the latest Disney films and the Bond movies, including *Live and Let Die*. In about 1973 or 1974, mum and dad bought our first colour television set, and we stopped going to the pictures after that. Mum would never miss *Crossroads* or *Coronation Street*.

On Saturday afternoon at 4 p.m. *World of Sport* would show wrestling. The programme cleared the streets. If you were in town everyone would rush back to see the

My favourite wrestler, Les Kellett, being stomped on by Johnny Creslaw. Of course, it was all put on, but we believed it back then. People would shout at the telly in anger if they thought someone wasn't fighting fair.

wrestling on TV. The wrestlers of the day included Les Kellett, Jackie Pallo, Mick McManus and the Royal Brothers. During some shows an older woman, complete with handbag, would climb out of the audience and start attacking the wrestler that she thought wasn't fighting fairly. Later wrestlers of the 1970s included Kendo Nagasaki (who always wore a mask), Giant Haystacks, Big Daddy (whose real name was Shirley Crabtree) and Steve Veidor.

On Saturday evenings there would be *The Generation Game* with Bruce Forsyth. It was very popular and attracted millions of viewers. The show involved getting contestants to take part in all sorts of activities from making pots, decorating cakes and baking bread. The winner got to sit in front of a conveyor belt with prizes on it, and had to memorise as many as they could at the end of the show to win them. Typical prizes included Teasmades, fondue sets, dinner services and, of course, a cuddly toy! Bruce Forsyth's glamorous assistant in the seventies was Anthea Redfern, who he went on to marry.

Saturday's TV also included the awful *Seaside Specials*, which showed Gerry Cottle's *Big Top* being filmed at various seaside locations. It had lots of viewers back then, but perhaps this was because nothing else was on. Regular acts included Little and Large, Keith Harris and Orville, Lena Zavaroni, Bernie Clifton, Showaddywaddy, The Wurzels, Sacha Distel, Peters and Lee, and The Goodies.

It's a Knockout ran from 1966 to 1988 but seemed at its most popular during the 1970s. Teams from around the country (sometimes the world) would compete in games in which they would wear large foam rubber suits in the shape of things like leprechauns, giants or other strange characters.

It inevitably ended up with the contestants getting soaking wet, much to the delight of its presenter, Stuart Hall.

At the beginning of the 1970s there were endless cowboy shows, but slowly detective series took over. Who could forget *Columbo, Shaft, Madigan, Kojak, Banacek, Cannon, The Rockford Files, Harry O, McLeod, Hawaii Five-O, McMillan and Wife, Barnaby Jones, Tenafly, Baretta, Quincy* and *Police Woman*. I'm sure that there were many more. The BBC had their own detective shows like *Dixon of Dock Green* and later *Shoestring* and *Hazell*, but they were never quite the same.

I remember a typical episode of the *Rockford Files*. Someone would break into Rockford's trailer, mess it up a bit, punch Rockford, and then there would be various cars following each other. Every episode followed much the same theme.

Harry O was very similar. What was unbelievable was that he lived on the beach and had Farrah Fawcett living upstairs but never showed any interest in her. Like Petrocelli, he had an unfinished project. Petrocelli worked on his house throughout the series and Harry O worked on his boat. Neither improved from week to week.

TV is certainly faster paced today but I still think I prefer the old stuff. Indeed, perhaps one of the best remembered 1970s detective shows was *Starsky and Hutch*. Everyone loved the show. I even got my mum to knit me a Starsky jumper. There were several people in the area that added white stripes to their red Fords so it would look more like Dave Starsky's car. Everybody would be in on a Saturday night, both adults and children, to see the latest episode. When David Soul came to Britain to make a film quite near our home, everyone went out to watch. I never did see

One summer, also in about 1975, we went to Pontins and I got to meet Jackie Pallo. Wrestling was incredibly popular at the time. He was just walking with his son to the nearby chalets so we had a chat with him and got both their autographs. He had his hair in a ponytail, and I remember thinking that he was a lot shorter than he looked on the telly. He was lovely to us.

him, but the local record shop managed to get some signed albums and I got one of those for Christmas.

Britain had its own popular detective shows, including *Jason King* early on and later, *The Sweeney* and *The Professionals*. The second two were both very well watched but they never had the same appeal as the American shows for me. *Jason King* summed up the fashions of the early 1970s with his loud shirts, cufflinks, cravats, wild hair and odd moustache.

Another very popular show of the later 1970s was *Happy Days*. At the time, the Fonz was the coolest person around. There were posters, t-shirts and badges everywhere saying things like 'Be Cool'.

A sticker given away free with Smith's Crisps. For a while, the Fonz and *Happy Days* seemed to be everywhere.

For a while, during the 1970s, the 1950s made a comeback. There were many fifties' songs in the charts, together
with teddy boy bands such as Showaddywaddy and Mud.
Everyone was listening to Buddy Holly, Elvis, Jerry Lee
Lewis and other stars of the fifties. The 1970s is remembered
mainly for glam rock and punk, but 1950s music played a
big part.

Shows like *Bilko* were also repeated. I loved *Bilko* but it
was always on after bedtime. I had a radio, which would not
only pick up shows from all over the world but would also
pick up the TV. So I would turn it down low when I went
to bed, turn off the lights and listen to it under the bedcov-
ers. I don't think mum and dad ever realised.

Other later 1970s shows included *Mork and Mindy*, which
was a spin-off of *Happy Days*. Robin Williams played Mork
from the planet Ork and his catchphrase 'Nanu Nanu' was
repeated by kids and adults worldwide.

There wasn't a kid in the land that didn't look forward
to the Christmas edition of the *TV Times* and the *Radio
Times*. We all used to go through it page by page to see what
would be on. Popular Christmas shows from 1970 included
The Morecambe and Wise Christmas Special, *Top of the Pops*,
Billy Smart's Circus (I didn't enjoy it even back then), *The
Black and White Minstrel Show*, *The Rolf Harris Show*, *It's a
Knockout!* and *The Cliff Richard Show*.

BBC shows for adults that we watched and enjoyed
included *The Survivors*, *Upstairs Downstairs*, *The Onedin Line*
and *That's Life* with Esther Rantzen.

Early 1970s children's TV shows that were enjoyed by
the family included *Pardon My Genie*, *Robert's Robots* and
Rentaghost. *Pardon My Genie* starred a genie, played by

Hugh Paddick, who was summoned up by Hal Adden, who worked in a hardware shop and was employed by Mr Cobbledick, played by Roy Barraclough. Later on, another actor, Arthur White, played the genie.

Robert's Robots featured an inventor, Robert Sommersby (played by Clive Banks), who built robots that would wander off and get up to all sorts of adventures. By far the best of the robots was the silver-faced KT (or Katie) who was played by Brian Coburn. His catchphrase, 'I like it Mr Sommerby', was repeated by kids in the playground all over the country.

Rentaghost was a very popular BBC series and went on for about eight years, well into the 1980s. The show featured many ghosts, the most memorable being Timothy Claypole, a mischievous jester, who was played by Michael Staniforth. All these children's programmes were written by Bob Block, who had great success in the 1970s and kept many kids all over Britain entertained.

The Tomorrow People was hugely successful. It began in 1973 and continued until 1979, with various cast changes over the years. Perhaps the best remembered cast members are the ones from the first series, which featured Nicholas Young (who played John), Peter Vaughan-Clarke (who played Stephen) and Sammie Winmill (who played Carol).

A few children's TV programmes stick in my mind from the later 1970s. We all loved *The Multi-Coloured Swap Shop* with Noel Edmonds, Keith Chegwin, Maggie Philbin and John Craven. On some Saturdays I would stay in bed and not get up until the whole programme had finished at 12.30 p.m. (I had the old black and white TV in my bedroom by then). All the kids loved the cartoon *Hong Kong Phooey!*, and also enjoyed entering the many competitions that were featured throughout the show. I don't remember anyone I knew ever winning, though. *Tiswas* with Christ Tarrant and Sally James was on at the same time on ITV, and was well watched. Its title officially stood for Today Is Saturday, Watch And Smile.

Many TV shows for children were continually repeated over the 1970s, including short five-minute shows before the evening news, like *The Magic Roundabout*, *Captain Pugwash*, *Paddington* and *Rhubarb and Custard*, etc. Some were made before the 1970s, but continued to be shown. Shows such as *Mr Benn*, *Fingerbobs*, *Noggin the Nog*, *Ivor the Engine* and *Bagpuss* were all shown in the afternoon.

When we got home from school, *Michael Bentine's Potty Time* would be on, which always featured puppets with peculiar voices and an invisible flea circus, with the fleas riding bikes and doing other tricks.

Doctor Who remained a favourite throughout the 1970s, and indeed still is today. In the early part of the decade, Jon Pertwee was the Doctor and was very popular. I found some of the episodes scary back then, and some even gave me nightmares, especially the ones featuring the Daleks or The Master. When Tom Baker took over the role, a whole new craze started for the programme.

Quiz shows and talent shows were also well liked. Everyone watched *Opportunity Knocks* with Hughie Green and his clapometer. Some of the acts were excellent, while some were terrible. Memorable acts from the show included Su Pollard, Paul Daniels, Middle of the Road, Mary Hopkin, Bonnie Langford, Les Dawson, Royston

Vasey (later Roy 'Chubby' Brown), Little and Large, Bobby Crush, Berni Flint, Tony Holland, Millican and Nesbitt, Neil Reid, Peters and Lee, Lena Zavaroni, Max Boyce and Frank Carson. *Opportunity Knocks* relied on audience participation to decide who won, whereas *New Faces*, its rival, had a team of judges who marked the acts. Famous acts to appear on *New Faces* included Patti Boulaye, Marti Caine, Lenny Henry, Michael Barrymore, Roy Walker, Victoria Wood, The Chuckle Brothers, Roger De Courcey and Nookie Bear (ventriloquist acts were much more popular then), Showaddywaddy, Jim Davidson, Gary Wilmot and many others. Dave Allen won one of the shows when it was originally shown on the BBC.

Kids loved magic in the 1970s and there were many magic tricks available from joke shops. Acts like Harry Corbett and Sooty, and Ali Bongo performed some magic on the TV, but when Paul Daniels appeared on the BBC, magic suddenly became very popular. There were books showing you how to perform tricks (both Paul Daniels and Michael Bentine produced one), as well as special magic card packs and Paul Daniels magic sets. The US had *The Magician* with Bill Bixby, while in Britain we had *For My Next Trick* with Paul Daniels.

The Golden Shot was another well-loved programme. It always followed *The Flaxton Boys* at Sunday teatime and was ruined by the thought that Sunday would soon be over and I'd be back to school the next day. It was hosted by Bob Monkhouse and was later taken over by Norman Vaughan and Charlie Williams. The shows are also remembered for Bernie the Bolt and Anne Aston, who added up the contestants' scores.

There seemed to be many sci-fi shows on during the 1970s. As well as *Doctor Who*, the BBC turned out *Blake's 7*. I was never a fan and only the scenery seemed more wooden than the acting. America churned out many sci-fi shows after the success of *Star Wars*. These included *Battleship Galactica*, *Buck Rogers in the 25th Century*, *Logan's Run* and *Planet of the Apes*. There were many shows about superheroes as well, including *Spiderman*, *The Six Million Dollar Man* ('Steve Austin, astronaut. A man barely alive'), *The Bionic Woman* (featuring Lindsay Wagner) and *The Incredible Hulk*, with Bill Bixby as Dr David Banner ('Don't make me angry, you wouldn't like me when I'm angry').

Other well-loved evening US shows included *The Man From Atlantis* with Patrick Duffy, *Wonder Woman* with Lynda Carter, *Chips* and *Charlie's Angels* with Farrah Fawcett, Kate Jackson and Jaclyn Smith. Posters of Farrah Fawcett in a red swimsuit appeared everywhere. Many were given away with copies of *The Sun*.

There were also many US comedies, such as *The Odd Couple*, which was based on the Jack Lemmon/Walter Matthau movie but featured Jack Klugman (Quincy) and Tony Randall. And there was *Rhoda*, which starred Valerie Harper and was a spin-off from the equally popular *Mary Tyler Moore Show*. *Rhoda* starred Julie Kavner as Rhoda's sister, Brenda, who is now well known for providing the voice of Marge Simpson.

Dallas became a television phenomenon in the 1970s. It started in 1978 and continued until 1991. When JR was mysteriously shot, car stickers, t-shirts and mugs appeared with the slogan: 'Who Shot JR?' In those days, everything was kept under wraps. The film canisters were flown from the US to England under high security and no one knew who the culprit was until the show was broadcast. It would be impossible to keep a secret like that nowadays.

There were so many other shows that we all loved and watched in the 1970s, including *The Muppets*, *MASH*, *The Waltons* (which was hugely popular at the time), *Taxi*, *Hart to Hart* with Robert Wagner, *The Love Boat*, *Benson*, *Soap* (it used to have me in stitches), *SWAT*, *The Life and Times of Grizzly Adams* (we all watched it at Saturday tea-time), *The Gemini Man* with Ben Murphy, *The Invisible Man* with David McCallum, *The Magician* with Bill Bixby, *The Ghost and Mrs Muir* with Hope Lange and Edward Mulhare, *Anna and the King* with Yul Brynner and Samantha Eggar, *Alias Smith and Jones*, *Daniel Boone*, *Police Story*, *The Barbary Coast* with William Shatner, *Switch* with Robert Wagner, *The Streets of San Francisco* with Karl Malden and Michael Douglas, *Hawaii Five-O* with Jack Lord ('Book 'em, Dano!'), *Quincy* with Jack Klugman, *Barnaby Jones*, *Baretta*, *Serpico*, *Simon Locke* and *Vegas*, etc. They certainly don't make television programmes like that anymore.

There were many excellent cartoons on the telly in the 1970s. As a boy, I loved them all. Many that were shown at the time had been made in the 1960s, such as *Tom and Jerry*, *Bugs Bunny*, *Arthur*, *Milton the Monster*, *The Flintstones* and *Top Cat*. *Top Cat* was renamed *Boss Cat* in the UK because a cat food brand was already called 'Top Cat' and they didn't want to give it any free advertising. There was *Journey to the Centre of the Earth* where a group followed the trail of Arnie Saccnuson to the core of the earth and to the lost

Kingdom of Atlantis. Recently, my parents were decorating my brother's old bedroom and they wondered why there were the letters 'AS' written on the wall in pencil. I remembered writing it on there forty years ago. 'AS' stood for 'Arnie Saccnuson' and the hidden letters showed the way to the centre of the earth!

The 1970s had a whole range of new cartoons, though. Our favourite had to be *Scooby Doo*. The show seems to have been made continuously ever since, sometimes with different characters like Scrappy, but there was nothing like the original cartoon series. The story would usually follow Freddy, Thelma, Valerie, Shaggy and Scooby as they stumbled across an old town in which part of it was meant to be haunted. In the end, the ghost would turn out to be the local police chief or mayor trying to scare people away in order to somehow develop the land. When the villain was caught, he would always say: 'And I would have gotten away with it if it wasn't for those pesky kids!' Well, that's how I remember it anyway.

Another well-loved cartoon of the 1970s was *Wacky Races* in which every week Dick Dastardly and Muttley would try to win the race by sabotaging the other contestants, who included the Slag Brothers, the Gruesome Twosome, Professor Pat Pending, Red Max, Penelope Pitstop, Sergeant Blast and Private Meekley, the Ant Hill Mob, Lazy Luke and Blubber Bear, Peter Perfect and Rufus Ruffcut and Sawtooth. *Wacky Races* was really a late 1960s cartoon but was shown throughout the 1970s. It led to a later spin-off featuring Penelope Pitstop and the Ant Hill Mob called *The Perils of Penelope Pitstop*. Dastardly and Muttley also had their own spin-off show called *Dastardly and Muttley in their Flying Machines*, which was also known as *Stop the Pigeon*.

Another Hanna-Barbera cartoon of the seventies was *Help! It's the Hair Bear Bunch!* which was made in 1971. It featured three bears – Afroed (the fast-talking Hair Bear), Bubi Bear and the more laid-back Square Bear. They all lived at the Wonderland Zoo and were always looking for ways to escape to embark on get-rich-quick schemes or to have a night of fun. Their enemies were the zookeeper, Mr Peevly, and his hapless assistant, Lionel J. Botch. Kids in the playground the next day would always be repeating Botch's catchphrase, 'Ooh! Ooh! Mr Peevly', especially in class when something went wrong. It didn't always go down well with the stricter teachers.

The Hair Bears had their own invisible motorcycle and they always managed to get back to their cage, which contained a concealed luxury bachelor pad, before Peevly and Botch could catch them.

In 1972, *Wait Till Your Father Gets Home* was made. We all loved it as kids but it seems that it was made as a cartoon aimed more at adults in America. The voice of the main character, Harry Boyle, belonged to Tom Bosley, who would later star as Mr Cunningham in *Happy Days*. The show featured Harry's wife, Irma (who was voiced by Joan Gerber), daughter Alice, who was a teenaged women's libber, and two sons, Chet and Jamie. Ralph Kane was their right-wing neighbour who was obsessed by conspiracy theories.

Other popular Hanna-Barbera cartoons of the 1970s included *Josie and the Pussycats*, *The Harlem Globetrotters*, *The Pebbles and Bamm-Bamm Show* (a spin-off from *The*

Flintstones) and *Hong Kong Phooey*. There were other cartoon shows made by the company, but many of them
weren't shown in the UK.

We all loved watching *The Harlem Globetrotters* long
before any of us had ever played basketball. Most kids didn't
even know that the show was based on real people. It had
a storyline similar to an episode of Scooby Doo, mixed in
with winning a game of basketball. We all knew at least
one of the characters from the show – some kids could
recite them all – but the only one that I remember was
Meadowlark, which was the nickname for the Globetrotters
player, George Lemon. However, other characters in the
show were Freddie 'Curly' Neal, Hubert 'Geese' Ausbie,
Pablo Robertson, J.C. 'Gip' Gipson and Bobby Joe Mason.
I think that the cartoon version of *The Harlem Globetrotters*
was the first introduction that British kids had to the game
of basketball, and when we were told that we could play the
game in the first year at our new school, we all jumped at
the chance.

There were also cartoons of the Jackson 5 and the
Osmonds. The Osmonds Cartoon ran between 1972 and
1973. The shows were incredibly similar. The Jackson 5
cartoon (called *Jackson 5ive*) lasted a bit longer, running
between 1971 and 1973. They had all sorts of adventures,
including being drafted, shrunk to miniature size, meeting
pirates, building robots and growing a beanstalk and meeting a giant. Uncannily, although the show was total fiction,
some of the episodes seem to have almost come true in
later years!

Another popular cartoon of the 1970s was *The Pink
Panther*, made by Mirisch films and DePatie-Freleng

Enterprises. Everyone enjoyed watching it. It was ruined in later years when the panther started talking and a laughter track was added.

There were certainly some great cartoons in the 1970s, which have since been imitated but never bettered.

Thirteen

ADVERTS

The first advert that I remember from the 1970s was the one for Coca Cola, which included the song, *I'd Like to Teach the World to Sing*. The song was later a number one hit for The New Seekers. Other famous adverts included the Hovis ad, where a boy pushes his bicycle up a cobbled hill. Everyone remembers the line, 'It was a grand ride back though!'

There were many public information films and adverts aimed at children. Road safety adverts included ones featuring Tufty (which were made in the 1960s) and a series featuring the Green Cross Man who was played by David Prowse (later Darth Vader in the *Star Wars* films). David Prowse made all the Green Cross Code adverts in 1975, but then in 1976 the advert featured other stars of the day, including Kevin Keegan, Joe Bugner, Les Gray from Mud and Alvin Stardust. David Prowse's catchphrase in the ads was, 'I won't always be there when you cross the road, so always use the Green Cross Code!'

Unigate Milk adverts featured stars like Muhammad Ali, Rod Hull and Emu, Sid James, Barbara Windsor and Frank Muir, all warning you to 'Watch out, watch out, there's a Humphrey about!' Kids would sing the song at school and milkmen would give away free badges and stripey straws like the ones shown in the adverts.

Frank Muir also appeared in the Cadbury's Fruit and Nutcase adverts in 1975, one of which showed a Scotsman tossing a caber.

Terry Scott at one time played an oversized school-boy eating his Curly Wurly in a series of adverts. The best remembered was the one in a museum, which featured the tag line, 'Outchews everything for 3p'. The PG Chimps featured in some of my favourite adverts of the 1970s. A memorable one showed the chimps as removal men, with the classic lines such as, 'Cooee, cooee Mr Shifter. Light refreshment', and 'Dad, do you know the piano's on my foot? You hum it, son and I'll play it'. Others portrayed the chimps as plumbers ('Pass the monkey wrench!'), wedding guests, safe breakers (featuring the voice of Bernard Bresslaw) and competitors in the Tour de France (with catchphrases, 'Can you ride tandem?' and 'Avez Vous Un Cuppa?').

There were many other classic adverts from the 1970s. Most people will remember the Cadbury's Smash advert, which aired in 1974. Smash was launched in the 1960s, but really took off after an advert appeared showing tin martians observing humans making mashed potato from their space-ship – they all rolled about laughing because the humans weren't using Smash. The tag line for the advert was, 'For Mash get Smash'.

The Milk Tray advert was very James Bond with a man jumping off tall buildings, leaping into speed boats and falling from helicopters, all to deliver a box of Cadbury's Milk Tray, with the tag line, 'And all because the lady loves Milk Tray'. Nimble's 'She Flies Like a Bird' advert featuring a hot-air balloon was shown often ('Nimble – real bread, but lighter'). Jimmy Savile appeared in an advert with the tag line, 'Clunk Click Every Trip', which was a road safety campaign to promote wearing a seatbelt. Wearing seatbelts soon became compulsory.

Other regular ads featured Intercity, Tufty the road safety squirrel, Ben Sherman shirts, Birdseye beefburgers, British Telecom's Busby ads (voiced by Bernard Cribbins), Campari (featuring Lorraine Chase), Corona Orangeade (using a Bilko-type voice as the bubbles pass their 'fizzicle'), Cresta (featuring a bear doing a good impression of Elvis with the tag line 'It's frothy, man'), Yorkie (with the Yorkie trucker), Marmite ('the growing up spread'), *The Sun* (with the voice of Christopher Timothy – 'It's all in *The Sun* this week!') and Unigate with Benny Hill playing a milkman.

Every ad break seemed to have an advert for a product promoted by K-Tel, who brought out a lot of LPs featuring compilations of love songs, country hits and rock 'n' roll heartbreakers. I'm sure that I've still got a few of their LPs somewhere. As well as K-Tel, there was also Ronco. Both produced a lot of gadgets, especially around Christmas time. These included 'The Clever Cutter', which cut vegetables, an iron for ironing your curtains while they were still up, a tool ('the BeDazzler') that put rhinestones all over your denim jackets and jeans or anything else, the 'Record selector', that allowed you to find the gap where your record came from, the 'Dial-O-Matic', that also allowed you to slice vegetables, and the 'Record Vacuum' to remove all that unwanted dust from the grooves of your records. All of these products seemed wonderful to us back then.

There were also TV adverts encouraging people to go into mining or to emigrate to Australia, and all you had to do was fill in the coupon in the *TV Times*.

Pepsi had an excellent advert in 1974 which contained the catchphrase, 'Lipsmackin' thirst quenchin' ace tastin' motivatin' good buzzin' cool talkin' high walkin' fast livin' ever givin' cool fizzin' Pepsi!' The advert featured Mike Grady trying to chat up two bikini-clad girls by offering them a Pepsi, only to find that they only spoke Swedish. A later Pepsi advert tied in with the revival of the 1950s and had a teddy boy (actor Peter Blake) singing *Summertime Blues*.

As a kid, the adverts I enjoyed most were the ones leading up to Christmas featuring all the toys we'd be pestering our parents (or Santa) for over the following month. They looked fantastic on TV and must have sold in their millions due to those wonderful ads. Classic Christmas adverts that I can remember are the ones for Action Man, Slinky, Rocket Racers, Haunted House, Operation, Monopoly, Buckaroo and Ker-plunk!

Another game which looked like it might be more interesting than it was, was Mastermind. I'm not sure if it was based on the television show or not, but it probably wasn't.

It was a code-breaking game that you would only play if you really had nothing better to do, although it always seemed popular.

There were also lots of adverts featuring moustachioed men advertising products like Cossack Hairspray for Men. I can't remember men using hairspray at all in those days, but they seemed to sell a lot of it. I remember one kid wearing it to school (he was the only one), and he got the mickey taken out of him all day. Men (and boys) were meant to smell like men and not girls, which is why they had products like Wright's Coal Tar Soap. Things must have changed, though, because there were products like Brut 33 aftershave advertised by sportsmen such as Henry Cooper ('Splash it All Over'), Barry Sheen and Kevin Keegan. If you got Brut 33 for Christmas, you knew it was coming because it smelled so strong that it even made its way through the Christmas wrapping paper! Another aftershave with a crazy advert was Hai Karate, which featured a man (quite often looking like George Roper from *Man About the House*) who, when he wore Hai Karate, found himself being pursued by Valerie Leon and had to fight her off with karate chops. Their slogan was, 'Be careful how you use it!' There were similar products like Denim and Blue Stratos that were equally as smelly.

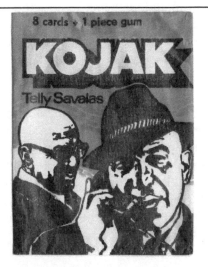

Fourteen

MOVIES

There were some great movies in the 1970s. Alan, for a
while, took me to the Saturday morning picture show at
the Drake Cinema in town which featured lots of adventure serials and a couple of films. I never found out how
the serials ended though because Alan, due to our five-
year age difference, decided that he would rather go with
friends of his own age. We did go to the pictures together
quite often, however, and I remember one time we went
to see *Battle of Britain* which starred Kenneth More, Trevor
Howard and Michael Caine. War films were very popular
and there were a lot of war stories in comics such as *Valiant*
for older boys.

The films that I remember from 1970 included *The
Aristocats*, *MASH* and *The Railway Children*. Mum and

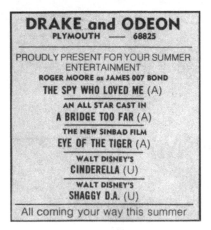

An advert in the local paper for my favourite cinemas, The Drake and The Odeon. I think that I saw every one of these films at the time, apart from *Cinderella*, which I'd seen earlier as a small boy when we lived in Singapore. Disney films were very popular at the time. From the movies shown, the year must have been 1977.

dad took us to see Walt Disney's *The Aristocats* at the local cinema and we loved it. It was very popular at the time and there were many free gifts given away with cereal. Long before the TV series, the film *MASH* was made. The film was an 'X' so I never got to see it, but Alan had a copy of the paperback so I read that some time later. I remember all the posters for the film, but it was some years before I actually saw it. I loved the film adaptation of *The Railway Children*, too, and had watched the series that was on TV in the late 1960s. There were probably many more famous films of 1970, but these are the ones that I had some sort of connection with.

1971 saw movies like *Diamonds are Forever, Bedknobs and Broomsticks, Dirty Harry, Fiddler on the Roof, Shaft* and *Willy Wonka & the Chocolate Factory*. We all loved James Bond but, from what I can remember, we all found *Diamonds are Forever* very boring. Sean Connery returned to the role after George Lazenby appeared in *On Her Majesty's Secret Service*. *Bedknobs and Broomsticks* was another Disney film; we always went to see the latest Disney films although this wasn't one of my favourites. My mum and dad loved *Fiddler on the Roof*, and I'm sure we all went to see it at The State, which was a cinema close to where we lived. I don't know if we ever went to see *Shaft*, as I was probably too young, but I remember the very popular TV series that followed the movie. *Willy Wonka & the Chocolate Factory* was based on the book by Roald Dahl, which we had read at junior school. The other film I remember from that year was *Dirty Harry*. Again, it was X-rated so I didn't get to see it, but I remember all the trailers, posters and clips for the film which were shown at the time. It looked very exciting to a young boy.

1972 saw *Fist of Fury* with Bruce Lee, which was talked about a lot in the playground because of the popular TV series *Kung Fu* with David Carradine. I doubt that any kid I knew had actually seen it, but some pretended they had. The TV series encouraged many of us to take up judo, which seemed to be the only martial art available in Britain at the time. The closest I got to martial arts was a pair of 'judo' pyjamas.

The Godfather is also, surprisingly, another film that I've never seen. It must have been the biggest film of 1972, and there were posters everywhere and lots of information about it written in the newspapers. There were many comedians doing impressions of Marlon Brando on the TV and some of the kids copied them.

I remember seeing the *Poseidon Adventure* with Alan. We seemed to go and see a lot of disaster movies and there were certainly plenty of them in the early 1970s. This one was very exciting and had many big stars, including Gene Hackman, Ernest Borgnine, Roddy McDowall (who seemed to be in everything in the 1970s), Shelley Winters and Pamela Sue Martin (who was later in The Hardy Boys and Nancy Drew Mysteries which was very popular later in the decade). By 1973, kung fu had taken hold. Rather than posters of David Carradine on their walls, many kids had posters of Bruce Lee from the big film of that year, *Enter the Dragon*. There were many fold-out poster magazines of Bruce Lee at the newsagents, as well as many books about him and the movie.

No kid would have seen *The Exorcist*, but it was the most talked-about movie of the year. It was supposedly based on a true story and there were reports of people committing suicide after seeing it. The newspapers of the time had a field day, and many cinemas subsequently banned it, which appeared to just make it even more popular. Just reading about it in the paper or seeing bits about it on TV was enough to give us kids nightmares, which is probably why I've never seen it.

Live and Let Die was the last film that mum took me to before we got a colour TV. I remember her saying that if we were going to get a colour TV (they were very expensive at the time), we wouldn't be able to afford to go to the pictures as much. People said back then that they preferred Sean Connery to Roger Moore as James Bond, but I thought that Moore was great in the part, especially in *Live and Let Die*. It had one of the best ever Bond themes sung by Paul McCartney and Wings, and the film exuded seventies fashion, with lots of loud clothes, trouser suits, flares and platform shoes. I loved it!

Other memorable films for me that year included *Serpico*, *The Sting*, *That'll be the Day* and *Westworld*. Despite everyone talking about them at school, no one had seen them. My parents had the music to *The Sting* and played the record over and over, and dad had the book which I read after him. *Westworld* fascinated me because it contained robots. There were lots of clips from these films featured on *Film 73*, and I'd have loved to go and see them all, but there wasn't any way that we would pass for 18 unless I sat on Alan's shoulders! Some kids did get in, though. There was an escape exit around the back of the cinema and this would be opened by someone already inside so that they could let their friends in.

The popular movies of 1974 included *Death Wish*, *Herbie Rides Again*, *The Man with the Golden Gun*, *Stardust*, *Thunderbolt and Lightfoot* and *The Towering Inferno* (which wasn't shown in the UK until 1975).

I remember going to see *The Towering Inferno* with Alan. I was probably too young to see it, but they let me in anyway. There were some huge stars in the film, including Paul Newman, Steve McQueen, Faye Dunaway, Fred Astaire, Robert Vaughan, Robert Wagner and William Holden. All the films were double bills back then, but I can't remember what film was shown with it.

Stardust was very popular because it featured David Essex, but it was rated 'AA' which meant that you had to be over 15 to see it. Even so, there was plenty about it in pop magazines, newspapers and, of course, *Look-in*.

The year 1974 also saw the release of Gary Glitter's film, *Remember Me This Way*. I queued right around the cinema to see this film and most of the queue seemed to be boys of my age, which was about 12 or 13 at that time. However, standing next to us was an elderly lady, who, once we were in the cinema, sat right behind me. It soon became apparent that the film was absolute rubbish, and before long there were kids throwing stuff at each other and climbing over the seats and causing mayhem. I wanted to see the rest of the film, but couldn't hear a word of it. The old woman behind me also wanted to watch it, and she leaned forward and tapped me on the shoulder and said, 'You're the best behaved boy in the cinema'. Luckily, there was too much going on for anyone else to hear what she said so I wasn't too embarrassed. Meanwhile, at the back of the cinema, some boys were telling everyone that they'd lost their bus fare and were asking if anyone had any change. I think that elderly lady gave them a shilling, and by the time I left they had pockets full of change that they'd conned out of people. Nobody from the cinema told anyone to behave, quieten down or to leave, but I suppose they must have been used to the audience reaction from previous screenings.

I went to see every James Bond film as it came out, but I can't remember who I went with to see *The Man with the Golden Gun*. The evil villain, Scaramanga, played by Christopher Lee, not only had three nipples but also had a golden gun, which was constructed from a pen, a lighter, a cufflink and a cigarette case. Kids at school pretended to be James Bond, while the swottier kids tried to construct their own Golden Guns.

The big film of 1975 that everyone was talking about was *Jaws*. One kid said that his dad had taken him to see it and that someone had been eaten by a shark and their head

A *Film Review* magazine from 1975 advertising *The Towering Inferno*.

bobbed up in the water. That was enough to put me off! My friend John had seen it once and wanted to go again, but I didn't really fancy it. Kids at school had poster mags featuring sharks and shark attacks, and the daily newspapers printed every shark story that they could get their hands on. I didn't see the film for many years after that because it all sounded too gory. When I did finally see it on TV, when I was a lot older, I quite enjoyed it and have seen it many times since. Other films I remember from that year included *Death Race 2000*, *Escape to Witch Mountain*, *One Flew Over the Cuckoo's Nest*, *The Stepford Wives* and *Tommy*. *Tommy* was popular because of glam rock and it was advertised every time we went to the cinema. *Death Race 2000* featured David Carradine, and again, everyone at school was talking about it. I had simpler tastes and went to see *Escape to Witch Mountain* instead. At the time, I loved going to the pictures and watching anything to do with films, such as Barry Norman's programme on the BBC. I bought *Film Review* every month so knew all about the upcoming films and what was on, even though I was too young to see many of them.

There were many great films in 1976, but the ones I remember are *Carrie*, because of all the publicity that followed it in the newspapers, *Freaky Friday* with Jodie Foster (I loved Disney films back then), *Logan's Run* with Jenny Agutter (which later spawned a successful TV series), *The Omen* (another film with lots of press coverage) and *Taxi Driver* with Robert de Niro. Movies like *Carrie* and *The Omen* seemed to bring out every story in the papers that involved a haunting or a poltergeist. A house near to us was reported to have a poltergeist, and objects were said to have been thrown around the rooms. I think it transpired that the occupants were after a council exchange!

By far the most publicised film of 1976 was *Rocky*. Every cinema I went in had adverts for the movie, and it was much talked about on TV, in the papers and in film magazines.

Popular films of 1977 included *Airport 77, Annie Hall, Close Encounters of the Third Kind, New York, New York, Pete's Dragon, The Rescuers, The Rollercoaster, Saturday Night Fever, Smokey and the Bandit, The Spy Who Loved Me* and *Star Wars. Close Encounters of the Third Kind* renewed the interest in UFOs, and suddenly there was a surge in sightings. It was felt back then that any day we would make contact with an alien species, although of course it never happened. I remember going to see *Close Encounters* but I missed the beginning. In those days, you could get away with staying in the cinema and watching the film over and over again without anybody saying anything. To get my money's worth, and because I'd missed the beginning, I watched the movie again. *Saturday Night Fever* was incredibly popular, increased the interest in disco music and brought the Bee Gees into the charts at very regular intervals. The most anticipated and talked-about movie of the year, though, was *Star Wars*, starring Harrison Ford, Carrie Fisher and Mark Hamill. At the time I hadn't heard of any of them.

1978's big hits were *The Deer Hunter, Grease, Halloween, Jaws 2* and *Superman. Jaws 2* wasn't as bad as everyone remembers it, but the later *Jaws* films were pretty dreadful. *Superman* was long anticipated and much was said about Marlon Brando's $4 million pay cheque. Watching it in the cinema, it seemed long and drawn out, especially the parts with Brando in, but that was probably just so they could get value for their money!

Grease with John Travolta and Olivia Newton-John was incredibly popular in 1978, and songs from the movie featured in the charts throughout the year.

1979's big movies were *10* with Bo Derek and Dudley Moore, *Alien*, *Apocalypse Now*, *Dracula*, *Kramer vs. Kramer*, *Mad Max*, *Monty Python's Life of Brian* (which was banned from our local cinema), *Moonraker*, *Quadrophenia*, *Rocky II*, *Star Trek: The Motion Picture* and *The Jerk*. The movie I most wanted to see that year was *Star Trek*. By then, the TV show hadn't been made for about ten years and there was much anticipation about the new movie. Unfortunately, for me the movie was a big let down. A lot had changed over the previous ten years and the film seemed to rely more on its special effects, mainly because of the success of other big movies such as *Star Wars* and *Superman*. For me it was disappointing because it had lost its 'TV feel', and the actors had just grown too old. When I saw the film back then, William Shatner looked like an old man. Seeing him today in the same film, he looks quite young!

Fifteen

TOYS AND GAMES

Perhaps some of the best toys and games ever invented were produced in the 1970s. Space Hoppers were very popular in about 1971, and everybody seemed to have one. I would bounce mine up and down the living room or across the back garden. I remember when I first got it, Alan and I took it to the nearest garage to inflate it. All kids took their bikes and other inflatables to the garage to blow them up, but then it was decided that this was unsafe and all of us were stopped from going there.

I also remember the craze in the early 1970s where everyone seemed to have a toy called Clackers. It consisted of two balls on the end of a string which 'clacked' together, and kids would see how many times they could keep them 'clacking'. In the end, there were reports of them being dangerous and they were eventually banned. There were even items on *Blue Peter* about them. It was all pretty daft. It was claimed that you could be injured while using them or that they might explode. A test was shown putting one of the Clackers in a vice until it shattered, something that was never going to happen when in the hands of a 10-year-old kid!

There were other crazes for hula-hoops, push scooters and pogo sticks. Lots of kids had scooters at the time and could be seen pushing them up and down the pavements. Roller skates were also incredibly popular, mainly with girls.

Every kid seemed to have a magic set and a chemistry set. The magic set contained lots of tricks you could try out on your gran when she visited. I once told her that I could magic a box around the room. What I hadn't told her was that my hamster was underneath! She was scared of any small rodents, especially mice, but she soon got used to our hamster in the end. The chemistry set contained all sorts of powders, crystals, chemicals and, for some reason, a dead moth and butterfly. It also included a microscope. With all the science fiction programmes on the television, you could imagine mixing everything together and conjuring up another world or something similar (it never happened).

Board games were very popular. Everyone had a game of Monopoly or Mouse Trap in their house. Other well-loved games of the 1970s included Buckaroo (later copied with *Jaws*), Ker-plunk!, Subbuteo, Cluedo, Operation and Battleship.

There was also The Fastest Gun, Rebound, Escape From Colditz, Connect 4 and Haunted House. Every kid wanted Haunted House after it was advertised on the TV in the

This photo shows me bouncing up and down our back garden. Space Hoppers were never as good as they appeared in the adverts. The highest you could bounce was maybe a couple of inches, although I wanted to bounce over the fence!

early 1970s. I think it reminded everyone of Scooby Doo and of some of the ghostly goings-on in many of the comics of the day, such as *Whizzer and Chips*. Every Christmas always brought board games and annuals, and much of the day would be taken up playing the latest one. Some games certainly looked more interesting in the adverts than they were in real life.

I loved my Viewmaster, which took reels that showed you an image in 3D when you held it up to the light. The reels that I remember having were ones of *William Tell*, *Star Trek* and *Tom and Jerry*. There seemed to be reels for every popular film and TV show, as well as educational reels about various places around the world.

TV-related games included On the Buses, Dad's Army, the Bionic Woman, Planet of the Apes, The Six Million Dollar Man, Kojak and Star Trek.

Slinkys were also very popular. They were huge springs that could walk down the stairs. The adverts at Christmas made them look great fun. Every kid had one, although they would eventually get tangled up. There were smaller versions of the same toy called 'Springers'. However, once you'd made it walk down the stairs a few times, you realised that there was little more you could do with it.

Our rooms were set up with Rocket tracks featuring 'Rocket Racers' or Mattel 'Hot Wheels' tracks. The plastic track would stretch from one end of the room to the other with double loops, breaks, bridges and other stunts for our latest Hot Wheels cars to perform. The Rocket sets were red and the Hot Wheels ones were bright orange. The more track you had, the more you could do with it. Some tracks stretched right out into the garden.

Another popular toy was the Scalextric. Alan and I would spend hours racing cars round and round the tracks. The cars on the TV adverts seemed to go on forever, doing all sorts of tricks along the way. When we went to Butlins in 1970, there were big tracks that you could race on. They were never very good though, as the tracks must have been worn out by all the use they got at the time.

Simple toys kept kids very happy back in the 1970s. One of the cheapest toys were small coloured rubber balls which kids would bounce as high as they could. They were always getting lost and we would often find a few when we were out playing. At the time they were given away with cereal.

The Action Man was the must-have toy for every boy back in the 1970s. At the beginning of the decade they just had painted faces, but very soon they had flock hair, eagle eyes and even gripping hands so they could hold their rifles and other tools. Action Men seemed to be everywhere. As kids, we would be throwing them out of windows on para-chutes or having mock battles. There was a huge range of outfits for them, including guardsman uniforms, football kits, astronaut suits, sailor uniforms and many others. There were also tanks, jeeps and motorbikes.

Boys throughout the 1970s constructed Airfix models. Battleships and warplanes were very popular, but there were also kits for sports cars, spacecraft, motorbikes and historical figures. Many boys would spend hours indoors constructing the latest kit and the glue was always quite strong-smelling back then. Talented kids would paint their kits perfectly, but most of us just stuck on the transfers that came with them. I had many kits and some hung from the ceiling on pieces of thread.

This photo shows some of the toys and other stuff we had in the 1970s, including an Action Man, bubblegum cards, a Robertson's Golly, Esso World Cup coins, Shell 3D animal cards, cereal toys, Timpo Eskimos, Corgi vehicles, badges and a Slinky. There's also a signed Tom Baker photo and my Starsky and Hutch mug that I got for Christmas in about 1975.

Later, electronic toys included the very modern sounding stylophone, which was made famous by Rolf Harris. The toy had been created in the 1960s and featured on David Bowie's *Space Oddity*, but it wasn't until the 1970s that it really took off, selling approximately three million. I never had one, or wanted one, but I did have Rolf Harris' wobble board, which I would annoy everyone with. Mine even had a Rolf Harris painting of a kangaroo on the front.

Cowboy dolls were very popular at the beginning of the 1970s. There were lots of westerns on the TV, and this led to later Lone Ranger and Tonto dolls being released. I remember in about 1970 saving up for one of these dolls. The local toy shop, Edwards, had one advertised for 19/6 (which today is just under £1). I saved all my old pennies that I had for pocket money in a jar, and, when I had enough, I took them up to the shop and poured them onto the counter.

'That's mis-priced!' said the surly shop assistant. 'You can have the horse for 19/6 though!'

I didn't bother. What good was a horse without the cowboy? I gathered up my pennies, put them back in the jar and went back home.

Dinky Toys were collected by many kids, although they were very expensive. Dinky produced several toys from the TV show *UFO*, including Ed Straker's car and the Interceptor. I had them both. There were also Dinky Toys made of the Pink Panther's car and the Eagle spacecraft from *Space 1999*, as well as models of cars, buses, lorries and other vehicles.

Cereal toys were much sought after. Totem Heads and Historical Busts were given away free with Shreddies, Indian Chief busts were given away with Kellogg's Cornflakes, Aristocats, Tarzan, and Tom and Jerry stickers were given away with Cubs and Shreddies, and other cereals offered spinning tops, badges and all sorts of things. I loved all the free toys. There were also 'mail aways' on cereal packets where you saved the coupons and sent them away for a gift. Kellogg's Frosties offered lots of plastic models – many were excellent – and I remember Quaker's Puffa Wheat offering a UFO board game.

'Raving Bonkers' (also known as 'Rock 'Em Sock 'Em' in the USA) was another sought-after toy. It incorporated two battling robots within a boxing ring, and the aim was to knock the other robot's head off.

Evel Knievel reached the height of his popularity in the 1970s, and he was regularly featured on ITV's *World of Sport* programme. His stunts included jumping over thirteen double-decker buses and trying to leap over the Grand Canyon. This made him very popular with young boys in the early 1970s. Ideal brought out Evel Knievel's Stunt Set, which featured Evel, his motorbike, some track and a wall of fire for him to drive through.

When Tom Baker took over the role of Doctor Who, new toys were issued which featured the Tardis and the Daleks. All were very popular.

The first TV computer game came out in the 1970s. 'Pong' had long been a feature in arcades and was a type of ping-pong/tennis game. It wasn't very exciting, and there were just two 'bats' at either end of the screen with a ball in the middle. This all seemed amazing to us in the 1970s, actually having an arcade game on our TV set. There were a few settings on the console, which allowed you to play tennis, ping-pong or squash. To be honest, I couldn't see much of a difference between any of them.

Perhaps the simplest toys and games were the ones we came up with ourselves, like conkers, hide-and-seek, shove ha'penny (where we would throw halfpennies at a wall and the thrower of the closest one got the lot), 'tag' or 'it', or just re-enacting last night's television in the playground.

The first wave of the skateboard craze in the UK started in about 1977. Our local zoo was closed down and paved over before being reopened as a skateboard park. After a few years, the craze died off altogether, leaving the aban-

Tom Baker appearing as Doctor Who in the 1970s. Tom wrote a column for the paper *The Reveille*, which I would read every week. He was brilliant with fans of the show and would sometimes phone them up out of the blue just for a chat.

doned park empty thereafter. The craze reappeared many years later.

The 1970s was a fantastic time for new toys and games. Nowadays, most things are computerised and I'm sure that many of the older board games never get played. This seems a great shame, as when I was a kid they always played a big part in our Christmas entertainment.

Looking back now, the 1970s seemed a wonderful time to be a kid – lots of fresh air and playing out in the sun, great TV programmes, innovative music, as well as some of the best toys ever invented. And, with hindsight, perhaps school wasn't as bad as I imagined it at the time. I certainly miss the decade and wouldn't hesitate to live it all again!

Three skateboarders enjoying the new skateboarding craze which swept the country in the late seventies.

A cool skateboarder at the then new skateboard park, which had just been built on the site of the old Plymouth Zoo.

Sixteen

MEMORABLE 1970s EVENTS

1970

This year was remembered for many things, including Dana winning the Eurovision Song Contest with *All Kinds of Everything*. Concorde made its first supersonic flight travelling at 700mph. Paul McCartney announced the split of The Beatles and that he was producing a solo album. Elsewhere in the music world, Elton John's second album was his first to be released in America. Apollo 13 was launched in April, but, due to an oxygen failure, the crew had to abort the mission. In May, The Beatles released their twelfth and final album, *Let it Be*. On 18 June, the Conservative Party won the General Election and Edward Heath became Prime Minister. In June, Brazil beat Italy 4–1 to win the

World Cup. In August, the Isle of Wight Festival took place and featured acts like Jimi Hendrix, The Doors, Joan Baez, Jethro Tull, The Who and Chicago. By 18 September, Jimi Hendrix was dead from a suspected drug overdose. On 20 September, Luna 16 landed on the moon, taking samples before it lifted off the next day. Janis Joplin died in her hotel room on 4 October after a heroin overdose. On 12 October, President Nixon announced the withdrawal of 40,000 American troops from Vietnam.

1971

On 31 January, Apollo 14 lifted off from Kennedy Space Center for the third successful lunar mission, landing on the moon on 5 February. Decimalisation Day took place on 15 February, and both the UK and Ireland switched to decimal currency. On 28 February, Evel Knievel set a new world record when he managed to jump over nineteen cars on a motorcycle. The postal workers' strike, led by UPW General Secretary Tom Jackson, ended after forty-seven days on 7 March. Joe Frazier defeated Muhammad Ali at Madison Square Garden on 8 March. In April, over 500,000 people in the US protested against the Vietnam War. Arsenal won the FA cup on 9 May. The crew of the Russian Soyuz 11 spacecraft died after their air supply was lost because of a leaky valve. Jim Morrison was found dead in his bathtub in Paris on 3 July. The Apollo 15 mission was launched on 26 July, and on 31 July astronauts David Scott and James Irwin became the first to use the lunar rover. On 31 October, a bomb exploded in the Post Office Tower in London.

1972

30 January became known as 'Bloody Sunday' after four-
teen unarmed marchers were killed in Derry, Northern
Ireland. Launched from Cape Kennedy on 2 March, the
Pioneer 10 spacecraft became the first man-made satellite
to leave the solar system. The 1972 Summer Olympics were
held in Munich between 26 August and 11 September.
On 5 September, the Palestinian terrorist group Black
September murdered eleven Israeli athletes. Emerson
Fittipaldi became the youngest Formula One World
Champion on 10 September. Atari issued its first commer-
cial video game, 'Pong', on 29 November. On 7 December,
the last manned moon mission, Apollo 17, took off carry-
ing astronauts Eugene Cernan, Ronald Evans and Harrison
Schmitt. The mission landed on 11 December, and Eugene
Cernan became the last man to walk on the moon on
14 December.

1973

On 1 January, the UK, the Republic of Ireland and
Denmark entered the European Economic Community,
which later became the European Union. *The Last of the
Summer Wine* was first shown on the BBC on 4 January.
More people watched Elvis Presley's concert in Hawaii
on 14 January than had watched the moon landings. On
15 January, President Richard Nixon announced the end
of offensive action in North Vietnam. George Foreman
defeated Joe Frazier on 22 January to win the heavyweight

world boxing championship. On 27 January, the Vietnam War ended with the signing of the Paris Peace Accords. On 3 March, Tottenham Hotspur won the Football League Cup at Wembley after beating Norwich City. Pink Floyd released their album *Dark Side of the Moon* on 17 March. On 5 May, Sunderland won the FA Cup final. Skylab, America's first space station, was launched on 14 May. In the midst of the Watergate scandal, President Nixon announced, 'I am not a crook!' to 400 Associated Press editors on 17 November.

1974

On 8 February, the crew of Skylab returned to earth after a record eighty-four days in space. Hiroo Onoda, a Japanese Second World War officer, finally surrendered in the Philippines on 10 March. The Terracotta Army of Qin Shi Huang, dating from 210 BC, was discovered in Xi'an in China. Abba won the Eurovision Song Contest on 6 April with *Waterloo*. West Germany won the Fifa World Cup on 7 July. On 8 August, due to the Watergate scandal, President Richard Nixon offered his resignation. Gerald Ford became the new President of the United States on 9 August. The BBC launched Ceefax on 23 September. On 30 October, Muhammad Ali famously knocked out George Foreman in the eighth round in Zaire, and became heavyweight world champion. The fight became known as the 'Rumble in the Jungle'.

1975

On 1 January, work on the British end of the Channel Tunnel was abandoned. Margaret Thatcher became the new leader of the Conservative Party after defeating Edward Heath on 11 February. Aston Villa won the Football League Cup on 1 March. The Queen knighted Charlie Chaplin on 4 March. Bill Gates founded Microsoft on 4 April. Lord Lucan was found guilty, in his absence, of the murder of nanny Sandra Rivett on 19 June. America's Apollo and Russia's Soyuz spacecraft docked in orbit for the first time on 17 July. Muhammad Ali beat Joe Frazier in a boxing match in Manila on 1 October, which became better known as the 'Thriller in Manila'. Ross McWhirter, the co-founder of the Guinness Book of Records, was shot dead by the IRA on 27 November.

1976

The year was remembered for the long, hot summer and also for Concorde's first commercial flight, which took off on 21 January. Twelve IRA bombs exploded in the West End of London on 29 January. Harold Wilson resigned as Prime Minister on 16 March. Patty Hearst became famous worldwide after being found guilty of robbing a San Francisco bank. Brotherhood of Man won the Eurovision Song Contest for Britain with *Save Your Kisses For Me* on 3 April. On 5 April, after Harold Wilson's resignation, James Callaghan became the new Prime Minister. Iceland and the UK ended the Cold War on 1 June. The heatwave reached its peak in July, whilst drought conditions continued. On 4 July, Israeli commandos rescued 103 Air France hostages at Entebbe. The Summer Olympics began in Montreal on 17 July. On 5 August, Big Ben ceased to work and stopped running for nine months. The Viking 2 spacecraft landed on Mars on 3 September. On 25 September, U2 was formed after drummer Larry Mullen Jr requested members for a new band at his Dublin school. On 1 December, The Sex Pistols gave their now-famous four-letter-word interview on *The Bill Grundy Show*.

1977

On 20 January, Jimmy Carter became the 39th President of the United States. The Sex Pistols were sacked from their EMI record label on 27 January. Fleetwood Mac released *Rumours* on 4 February. The Clash's debut album was released on 8 April. On 1 May, the M5 motorway was completed. Queen Elizabeth II started her Jubilee tour at Glasgow on 17 May. A few days later, Manchester United won the FA Cup, and a few days after that Liverpool won the European Cup. *Star Wars* opened in the US on 25 May and was first shown in the UK on 27 December. From 6-9 June, Jubilee celebrations were held around the country. Kenny Dalglish became Britain's most expensive footballer after a £444,000 transfer on 10 August. The Space Shuttle made its first test flight on 12 August. On 16 August, Elvis Presley died aged 42 at his home in Memphis. A smaller £1 note was introduced on 23 August. On 16 September, Marc Bolan died in a car crash after his mini hit a tree.

On 26 September, Freddie Laker launched his budget airline Skytrain. Bing Crosby died on 14 October while playing golf. Charlie Chaplin also died, on Christmas Day.

1978

The Sex Pistols played their final show on 14 January. Two days later, the firefighters ended their strike. Anna Ford became the first female ITN newsreader on 13 February. On 22 April, Izhar Cohen and the Alphabeta with *A-Ba-Ni-Bi* won the Eurovision Song Contest. Evita opened in London on 21 June. Louise Brown became the first test-tube baby in July. Pope John Paul I succeeded Pope Paul VI on 26 August, but died only a few weeks later. On 7 September, Keith Moon, the drummer of The Who, died of a drug overdose. The soundtrack from *Grease* became the number one album on 7 October. On 16 October, Pope John Paul II succeeded Pope John Paul I. A bakers' strike led to many bakeries rationing bread in November.

1979

On 2 January, Sid Vicious stood trial for the murder of his girlfriend, Nancy Spungen. On 5 January, lorry drivers took strike action. In the US, *YMCA* became the Village People's only number one hit on 6 January. Rail workers took strike action for twenty-four hours on 15 January, which was followed by thousands of public workers striking and was later called the 'Winter of Discontent'. On

2 February, Sid Vicious was found dead in New York of a suspected heroin overdose. On 9 February, Trevor Francis signed Britain's first £1 million football deal to play for Nottingham Forest. A thousand schools closed on 12 February after a heating oil shortage due to the lorry drivers' strike. *Parallel Lines* by Blondie became the number one album on 17 February. Nottingham Forest won the Football League Cup in March. Margaret Thatcher became the country's first female Prime Minister on 4 May. Elton John became the first western musician to perform live in the Soviet Union on 21 May. Sebastian Coe set a new world record for running a mile in July. On 10 August, Michael Jackson released *Off the Wall*. The IRA assassinated Lord Mountbatten on 27 August. On 5 September, Manchester City paid £1,450,000 for the Wolverhampton Wanderers midfielder, Steve Daley. In November, bank rates reached an all-time high of 17 per cent. On 16 November, Anthony Blunt is named as the fourth man in the Cambridge Spy Ring. Rod Stewart's *Greatest Hits Vol. 1* became the last number one album of the decade.

Seventeen

WHATEVER HAPPENED TO?

TV Stars

Many of our favourite acts from the 1970s are no longer around, but some of the stars of the day still appear on TV. If you want to catch a glimpse of one of your best-loved stars of the seventies, just tune in to the latest soaps. Rudolph Walker from *Love Thy Neighbour* regularly appears in *Eastenders*, and his neighbour, Jack Smethurst, appeared in *Coronation Street* a few years back.

Andrew Hall (*Butterflies*) also recently appeared in *Coronation Street* and Jeff Rawle (*Billy Liar*) has appeared in numerous TV shows over the years, including, most recently, *Hollyoaks*. Occasionally, you'll be watching a show such as *Casualty* and think, 'Where do I recognise that actor from?'

Frank Carson, famous for being one of The Comedians, is now in his 80s and still tours; Bruce Forsyth, of course, still regularly appears on TV; Paul Daniels occasionally pops up on reality shows, as does Jimmy Savile.

I recently watched *Catweazle* on DVD and was amazed to find that everyone in the cast had died apart from Catweazle himself, who, at the time of writing, is 87.

American stars such as William Shatner and Lee Majors have both appeared in adverts for breakfast cereal, and Shatner often appears in US shows.

Numerous British stars are still regularly appearing on TV, including Robert Lindsay (*My Family*), Tom Baker, Dennis Waterman (*New Tricks*), Rolf Harris, Bill Oddie, Bernard Cribbens and Ronnie Corbett, etc.

Next time you're watching *Casualty* or *Holby City*, see how many you can spot!

Wrestlers

It has been a very long time since I met Jackie Pallo in 1975 and unfortunately, like most of the wrestlers we all loved back in the 1970s, he has now passed away. Jackie died in 2006. His autobiography, published in 1985, summed up wrestling perfectly and was called, *You Grunt, I'll Groan*. Other stars of the ring are also long gone, including Les Kellett (d. 2002), Brian Glover, who performed as 'Leon Arris, the Man from Paris' (d. 1997), Giant Haystacks (d. 1998), Big Daddy (d. 1997) and Pat Roach (d. 2004).

Some of those great wrestlers, however, are still around, including Kendo Nagasaki, who always appeared in the ring wearing a mask, and Mick McManus, who was billed as 'the man you love to hate'. It seems funny now that the streets would be empty at 4 p.m. because everyone was at home watching the wrestling. American-style wrestling took over, but it was never quite the same.

Toys

We all loved our Palitoy Action Man, but by 1984 production ceased and one of the best toys of the 1970s was replaced by the much smaller 'Action Force'. In 1993, Action Man returned as a muscle-bound poor imitation of its former self. A new generation played with them until 2006, but they could never compare with our original 1970s Action Men. Reproductions of Action Men were brought out for his 40th anniversary, but somehow they didn't look the same.

I loved bouncing around on my Space Hopper (called a 'hoppity hop' in the US) in the garden in 1970, but by the 1980s they had disappeared, although similar toys made by other companies appeared on the market. Today, it's possible to buy an adult-sized Space Hopper, just like the ones you had in the 1970s, from various outlets on the Internet.

Board games, for the most part, have disappeared and have been largely replaced with computer games. Monopoly, Scrabble and Chess are still about, but I can't imagine many kids of today being very happy with getting any of these for Christmas!

Many of the toy companies that we all knew in the 1970s have long since gone bankrupt. However, a quick search of the Internet reveals that you can still buy Slinkys, Clackers and even marbles, although they must all be bought by nostalgic people over 40 because I've never seen any kids playing with them.

Pop Stars

One of my favourite pop stars of the 1970s, Alvin Stardust, continues to tour and make records. Amazingly, many of our favourite bands and singers from that time are still touring the country, including David Essex, the Bay City Rollers (as Les McKeown's Legendary Bay City Rollers), The Rubettes and Slade (without Noddy Holder). Sweet have two bands: 'Andy Scott's Sweet', who tour the UK, and 'Steve Priest's Sweet', who tour the USA. Unfortunately, two members of Sweet are no longer around; these are Brian Connolly (d. 1997) and Mick Tucker (d. 2002). Hot Chocolate still tour but with a different line-up. Showaddywaddy also still tour and have appeared at Butlins, as well as other venues. There have been many 1970s tours over the years, which have included acts like Brotherhood of Man, the Glitter Band and, as mentioned earlier, Alvin Stardust.

Many groups now have touring tribute bands, including ELO, T. Rex, Queen, Thin Lizzy, Abba and Blondie (although the original Blondie are still going strong, even doing live performances for BBC radio).

David Bowie, Elton John, Bryan Ferry, Paul McCartney and many others continue to record new material. It's a shame that many stars from the 1970s, such as Marc Bolan,

Brian Connolly, Freddie Mercury, Phil Lynott, Les Gray and Bob Marley, are no longer around.

Chocolates and Sweets

Many of the sweets and chocolates that we loved in the 1970s disappeared forever a long time ago, but quite a few still survive, including Curly Wurlys, Mars Bars, Milky Bars, Crunchies, Wagon Wheels, Caramac, Galaxy and Flake. Some chocolates that I thought had disappeared are still for sale; these include Fry's peppermint cream, Fry's orange cream, Turkish Delight and Cadbury's Freddo bars. Some websites specialise in selling sweets from the 1970s, including flying saucers, bon bons, chocolate mice, sherbet lemons, Midget Gems, Sweet Tobacco, pear drops, liquorice wands, Toasted Teacakes, acid drops, Love Hearts, drumsticks and fizzers. It's probably an age thing, but none of them taste as good to me as they did when I was a kid in the 1970s.

CB Radios

CB Radios were an odd craze during the 1970s. Talking to each other, free of charge, seemed a much better idea than queueing up to pay for a call in a phone box. They died out in the 1980s, long before the Internet, mass-produced mobile phones or emails existed. Of course, they still continue to be used by truckers and other services, but they will probably never again have the same appeal that they once had in the 1970s.

Cars

Most of our favourite cars from the 1970s have long since disappeared, and can now only be seen in programmes such as *Life on Mars* or in old episodes of *The Professionals* or *The Sweeney*. Some cars have been redesigned and are still on our roads, such as the Mini and the Volkswagen Beetle. Of course, they're much more reliable, a lot less rusty and a lot more economical on petrol. Today, the only place to see a car from the 1970s is in a museum or at a car show. Occasionally, when the summer months come along, enthusiasts can be seen driving around in their old Vivas, Escorts and Capris.

The Ice Cream Man

The ice-cream man is still around, and occasionally I hear the sound of *Greensleeves* as he drives by. Most ice-cream vans seem to come from the 1970s and many are very colourful. A lot of them have their own private pitches and it's very rare to see one touring the streets, waiting for kids to queue up. Ice cream is mostly bought from superstores nowadays so in general people have no need to go to a van. There are many vans at popular holiday resorts, of course, but the days when we all shot up and ran to the front of our houses when we heard the chimes of the local ice-cream van are unfortunately long gone.

Playing Outside

Whatever happened to kids playing outside? I can't imagine anyone building a den nowadays. Of course, kids still ride their bikes and play outside, but not in the great numbers they once did in the 1970s. In the 1980s, there were more superior video games and this played a part in keeping a lot of kids indoors. Many more kids, for the first time, had their own TV sets in their bedrooms, and, with the introduction of the video recorder, could watch their favourite films without leaving the house. Of course, nowadays, with the Internet and computer games, more and more kids find all the entertainment they need at home.

In the 1970s, there was always an open building site with lots of materials available to build dens and no one would stop you from taking them. Today, however, with health and safety regulations and the fears of parents, doing someting like building a den in the woods would probably be discouraged.

Cereal Free Gifts and Other Giveaways

When I was a kid, I would make sure that mum bought a certain brand of cereal so that I could get the free gift inside. I would have collections of all sorts of things, including Red Indian heads, totem poles, cars, astronauts, animals, spinning tops and many other items. They used to be in every brand of cereal going, but then, for a while, there seemed to be nothing. Manufacturers were urged not to attract kids to sweet cereals by offering them free toys and, although free gifts were still given away with cereal after that, they never seemed as exciting as when I was 11.

We all collected Robertson's Gollys, but they eventually disappeared in 2002 because the company felt that children were no longer interested in them. Perhaps the true reason was that the gollys were seen to be racist, and books like *The Three Golliwogs* by Enid Blyton became *The Three Gollys*.

Brooke Bond cards were collected by just about every boy in Britain and contained sets about dinosaurs, space travel, cars, birds, fashion and flags. The series seemed to end in 1999 with a set called 'The Wonderful World of Kevin Tipps'. Most of the later collections are very forgettable, but the sets from the 1960s and 1970s are still memorable today.

Kids collected badges in great quantities in the 1970s, and they were given away with everything, including crisps, ice cream, chocolate, birthday cards, food and snacks. Badges don't appear to have the same appeal these days.

Adverts

Some adverts, like the ones for Hamlet cigars, would never be shown on TV again, but one long-running series of adverts, that many people miss, is the PG Tips chimp adverts. They never made me want to drink a certain brand of tea, but we all laughed at their antics and the fact that they talked. The chimps were briefly dropped in the 1970s after animal rights activists protested and sales fell. However, the chimps returned and the Tipps Family continued to entertain us until 2002. This made it the longest-running advertising campaign on TV (it started in 1956), and the Tipps Family now have their own Facebook page!

The chimps were replaced by the T-Birds, animated by the same company as Wallace and Grommit, but nowadays, Johnny Vegas appears in the adverts complete with a woollen monkey.

Other titles published by The History Press

A 1960s Childhood:
From Thunderbirds to Beatlemania
PAUL FEENEY

978 0 7524 5012 4
£8.99

Do you remember Beatlemania? Radio Caroline? Mods and Rockers? The very first miniskirts? After the tough and frugal years of the 1950s, the 1960s was a time of changed attitudes and improved lifestyles. With chapters and illustrations on home and school life, games and hobbies, music and fashion, this delightful compendium of memories will appeal to all who grew up in this lively era.

1970s London:
Discovering the Capital
ALEC FORSHAW

978 0 7524 5691 1
£11.69

London in the early 1970s was where the lights seemed to shine the brightest. Yet London was also a city struggling to find its post-war identity, full of derelict docklands, undeveloped bomb sites, demonic motorway proposals and slum-clearance schemes. Discover the decade which saw the three-day week, the Notting Hill riots and the last of the anti-Vietnam war protests.

How We Played:
Games from Childhood Past
CAROLINE GOODFELLOW

978 0 7524 4330 0
£15.29

Games are a huge part of childhood, and memories of specific games stay with us forever. From childhood pastimes of the Middle Ages through to street games of the 1950s and '60s and into the current decade; this book will awaken distant memories of childhood and transport the reader to another time. A nostalgic look at how we played.

Bats in the Larder:
Memories of a 1970s Childhood by the Sea
JEREMY WELLS

978 0 7524 5705 5
£8.09

When 11-year-old Jeremy Wells moved from London to the Sussex coast, he was scarcely prepared for the weird and wonderful world he would encounter; where goats used public transport, buses waited for people and trains didn't fit the stations. Affectionate and hilarious, this book recalls the culture shock of moving to an ancient town which was just two hours – and two decades – away from the capital.

Visit our website and discover thousands of other History Press books.

www.thehistorypress.co.uk